Aim Your Control, Control Your Aim.

How to be the parent you want to be, the parent your kids need you to be.

Andrea Martin-Pieler
M.Ed., C.P.C.C., M.O.M.

A PocketCoach Workbook

Aim Your Control, Control Your Aim.
How to be the parent your want to be, the parent your kids need you to be.
By
Andrea Martin-Pieler, M.Ed., C.P.C.C.

© Copyright 2003 by Andrea Martin-Pieler.
All rights reserved. Printed in the United States of America.
No part of this book may be reproduced, stored in a retrieval system, or transmitted by any means, electronic, mechanical, photocopying, recording, or otherwise, without written permission from the author, except for the inclusion of brief quotations
in critical articles and reviews.

Unattributed quotations are by Andrea Martin-Pieler

Library of Congress Control Number: 2003108614
ISBN 0-9742009-0-5

For further information, please contact the publisher:

Integrated Strategies
Brookfield, Illinois 60513-1525

Cover by Patrice Blackburn Design

Aim Your Control, Control Your Aim.

Part of the *A-ha Living* Series

A-ha's are the Insights we get when we Pay Attention.

This workbook provides the foundation for:

- Guided Independent Discovery -

- Individual Coaching –

- Family Coaching -

- Guided Group Discovery Workshops –

For more information:
andy@mycoachandy.com
www.mycoachandy.com

Contents

Acknowledgements, vi
Welcome to A-ha Parenting, vii
How to Use This Workbook, viii

SECTION 1 The Control Continuum — 1

The Dreaded Control Word, 3

A-ha 1:1 From Automatic Pilot towards Intentional Self, **5**
A-ha 1:2 Meet the Continuum, **7**
A-ha 1:3 A Demonstration of the Difference, **9**
A-ha 1:4 Parents Along the Continuum, **10**

SECTION 2 Kids and Control — 13

Understanding the Impact, 15

A-ha 2:1 Obstacles and Fallacies at the Illusion End, **17**
A-ha 2:2 The Beauty of the Reality, **24**
A-ha 2:3 A Bottom Line… Our Kids Get Really Scared, **29**
A-ha 2:4 Okay, An Admission, **30**
A-ha 2:5 Several Suspicious Characters, **31**
A-ha 2:6 Another Bottom Line… No Need to be Perfect, **37**

Kids and Control Check In, 39

SECTION 3 In Charge of Me — 41

Exploring Barriers, Expanding Perspectives, 43

A-ha 3:1 What Makes Shifting So Hard? **44**
A-ha 3:2 My Catch 22, **47**
A-ha 3:3 Paying Attention, **50**
A-ha 3:4 Either-Or, **52**
A-ha 3:5 Continuums: Busting Open Either-Or, **54**
A-ha 3:6 Shifts: Moving along Our Continuums, **61**
A-ha 3:7 Worrying IS a Choice, **66**
A-ha 3:8 Those Pesky WhatIfs, **67**
A-ha 3:9 Curb Your Impatience, **69**
A-ha 3:10 Clarify Your Intentions, **72**
A-ha 3:11 Be the Changes, **73**

In Charge of Me Check In, 75

Contents

SECTION 4 Create the Reality — 79

Prevention and Intervention, 81

Strategy 1 Shift to a Learning Stance, **83**
Strategy 2 Let them have it (the responsibility that is), **86**
Strategy 3 Put it on the table, **89**
Strategy 4 Stop the action and regroup, **91**
Strategy 5 Lighten up, **93**
Strategy 6 Let it go, **96**
Strategy 7 Pull the plug on non-productive patterns, **98**
Strategy 8 Assess the nag level, **100**
Strategy 9 Check in, check out, **102**
Strategy 10 Untangle the feelings, **104**
Strategy 11 Word problems, go figure! **107**
Strategy 12 Explain the bottom line, **109**
Strategy 13 Stop trying to fix & solve, just listen, **111**
Strategy 14 Just love 'em, **113**
Strategy 15 The butterfly and the bull, **116**
Strategy 16 Co-design, **118**
Strategy 17 Reframe it, **120**
Strategy 18 Use the back door, **124**
Strategy 19 *You're right, I can't make you*, **126**
Strategy 20 Turn off that automatic no, **128**
Strategy 21 Unscramble the issues, **130**
Strategy 22 Walk 13 steps in their Nikes, **132**
Strategy 23 Think smaller, **136**
Strategy 24 Hang in there, **138**
Strategy 25 Aim your control… Control your aim, **140**

Strategy Check List, 143

SECTION 5 Purposeful Structure — 151

Managing Structure, 153

A-ha 5:1 The Gray Area Factor, **155**
A-ha 5:2 Internal Structure, **157**
A-ha 5:3 Just Right, **160**
A-ha 5:4 Too Little Structure, **162**
A-ha 5:5 Too Much Structure, **163**
A-ha 5:6 The Primary Adjustment Tools, **168**
A-ha 5:7 The Feedback/Message Tool, **171**
A-ha 5:8 The Rules/Expectations Tool, **173**
A-ha 5:9 The Options Tool, **175**
A-ha 5:10 The Outcomes Tool, **177**
A-ha 5:11 What to Look For, **179**

A-ha 5:12 Questions to Ask Yourself, **180**
A-ha 5:13 Tying It All Together, **181**
A-ha 5:14 Four More Purposeful Structure Tips, **186**

Purposeful Structure Check In, 190

SECTION 6 Power Struggles · 192

Last but certainly not least, 194

P.S. 6-1 Avoiding Power Struggles, **195**
P.S. 6-2 Disengaging from Power Struggles, **200**
P.S. 6-3 A Power Struggle Check List, **206**

A Final Check In · 207

Acknowledgments

I am indebted to Jeff for the amazing editing job. He helped me clarify my intentions and remember that even when I write from the heart I need to use real words and something close to proper grammar.

I am grateful for all the wonderful parents, educators and kids I have worked with over the past twenty-eight years. My experiences with them are reflected throughout this **PocketCoach** workbook.

And I am profoundly thankful for Sarah and Katie, the daughters I have been blessed with. My experiences with them are reflected throughout everything I am, everything I do. Sarah and Katie have been fabulous teachers.

Over the years I have been delighted each time my daughters have said to me they want to 'mom' their children the way they have been 'mommed'.

Well guys, here's the manual…

I dedicate this book to Sarah and Katie with all my love.

Aim Your Control, Control Your Aim.

Welcome to A-ha Parenting

A-ha Parenting is being the parents we want to be, the parents our kids need us to be.

Yet life can be so hectic, especially as moms and dads. We get so caught up in taking care of business that there is barely time to breathe let alone think about how we are parenting our kids. We often know where we want to end up but have so little time to consciously create what's needed to get there. And sometimes we lose sight of where we are going altogether….

This **PocketCoach** workbook gives you a respite from life's hectic pace, from the busy-ness of being mom and dad, to discover what *A-ha Parenting* means for you and your kids. As you read, watch for **Irma** your **PocketCoach**. She'll ask you questions to check for understanding and to uncover your true beliefs and feelings. She'll help you connect with your unique wisdom and talents so they are available to your parenting. She'll help you discover your own A-ha's…

Irma asks a lot of questions! Don't get overwhelmed. Read thoughtfully and stay curious. Trust that you'll know which questions to spend the most time with.

Partner with **Irma** and reflect deeply. Do the exercises. Let your heightened awareness turn into effective action and your thoughtful action turn into increased awareness. The **PocketCoach** will help you integrate what's being offered so you can determine how to make it your own, so you can figure out how it will or won't work in different situations.

After all, you are the expert on your family. The more actively you partner with **Irma the PocketCoach**, the more you will get what you want out of this workbook.

Happy Discovery,
Andy Martin-Pieler

Aim Your Control, Control Your Aim.

How to Use This Workbook

At a Glance

Section 1 **The Basic Model**	Section 4 **Interacting With Our Kids**
Section 2 **How the Model Affects Our Kids**	Section 5 **Creating the Environment**
Section 3 **Clearing the Way for Ourselves**	Section 6 **Eliminating Unnecessary Battles**

Option 1: Start on page one and work through each section, A-ha by A-ha, question by question, and exercise by exercise.

    This option is ideal because each section in *Aim Your Control, Control Your Aim.* lays the foundation for subsequent sections.

Option 2: Get a general sense of what the workbook offers by simply reading the material in each section without addressing the questions and doing the exercises. Then choose a starting point for your in-depth exploration and discovery.

    This option may help you choose which components address your unique circumstances and priorities.

Option 3: Read all six Section Introductions and choose where to start.

    This is a viable option because each section can stand alone in helping you be the parent you want to be.

A note about Awareness and Action: All six sections contain both How-come's and How-to's. If you are looking for immediate action to take with your kids, sections four and six may be the place for you to start. Keep in mind, however, that sections one, two, three, and five will help you implement the strategies and steps.

Tips for getting the most out of this book

- ✓ Read with every intention to stop and reflect.
- ✓ Have something handy to write on.
- ✓ Don't hesitate to highlight and make notes in the book.
- ✓ Relate what you are discovering in the book to changes you notice in your own and your kids' responses. This will enhance the learning…

Section 1

The Control Continuum

Section 1: The Control Continuum

The Dreaded Control Word
The word that launched a thousand emotions!

We dislike being told we are controlling. It's overwhelming to hear, "You have no control." We fear our kids are out-of-control. We may feel guilty that we are such 'control freaks'. And we hate the thought of being controlled.

When it seems as if someone is trying to control us, we may resent their suggestions so much that we do the exact opposite even if we agree with them! (You might have noticed this with your kids too…)

There is such intensity attached to the concept of control. Yet control is a neutral concept. It's not good or bad. It is not all this or all that, useful or destructive. At times it is absolutely necessary and at times it is uncalled for, misguided, or too limiting. It depends on circumstances, methods, and **FOCUS**.

Because the concept of control triggers such strong feelings in both the controller and the 'controllee'- the parent and the kid, the kid and the parent- the Mother Lode of Expansion Questions[1] for parents is:

> "Where Do I Stand on the Control Continuum?"

According to Webster, control means "to exercise restraint or direction over; to hold in check, eliminate or prevent the flourishing of…"

The Control Continuum allows us to explore how we can get the biggest bang for our control bucks. It shows us what we should be **FOCUSING** on as we attempt to 'exercise restraint or direction over', what we should actually be trying to 'hold in check, eliminate or prevent the flourishing of…'

---

[1] Expansion Questions: Open ended questions that help people increase their awareness

Section 1: The Control Continuum

We are in control when we have true choice, when we are able to determine outcomes, and when we have say-so over the steps that realize these outcomes. We are in control when we are not being blindsided by unconscious beliefs, unrecognized emotions, or hidden agendas.

The Control Continuum shows us where to look for and find this control.

> **FAQ:** So is this workbook for parents who are too strict or for parents who are too lenient?
>
> **Aim Your Control, Control Your Aim.** is for parents who are *too* strict **and** *too* lenient. It is for parents who are 'too' anything.
>
> The adverb '*too*' indicates that something needs adjusting. The **PocketCoach** helps parents raise their awareness so they notice the '*too*'. And the workbook exercises and strategies help parents adjust their actions to eliminate the '*too*'.
>
> **Aim Your Control, Control Your Aim.** is for all parents who want to maximize the powerful influence they have with their kids in a way that is most beneficial to their kids.

- Name your '*too*'

    I am too…

    I am too…

    I am too…

- Describe how each one impacts your parenting.
- Now rewrite them without the '*too*'

    I am…

    I am…

    I am…

- Describe how each one of these impacts your parenting.
- Notice what happens when you eliminate the '*too*'.

A-ha 1:1

From Automatic Pilot towards Intentional Self

To discover where we stand on the Control Continuum we must turn off our **Automatic Pilot** and shift towards **Intentional Self**.

Automatic Pilot

Automatic Pilot means thinking, doing, and feeling the same things repeatedly because we haven't even realized what was going on. It is habit. It is unconscious patterns. It is not recognizing how we are making decisions, why we are responding the way we are. We don't notice so we have no choice.

It doesn't, however, just mean the same thing over and over again. Once we notice our thoughts, actions, and feelings, we may still choose to continue the same way. Automatic Pilot is about **unawareness** not **repetitiveness**. It is through recognition that we shift our beliefs and responses from Automatic to Intentional.

Intentional Self

Self-awareness, self-knowledge, the inner journey… Knowing who we are as people and as parents. Consciously choosing how we will interact with, provide for, and raise our kids. Intentional Self is noticing our feelings, beliefs and actions. It's being aware of how we are allocating our resources; our time, energy, and attention; and understanding how this impacts our decisions and our kids.

Shifting towards Intentional Self is what enables us to put into effect all the great parenting information available to us…

> You know how it is. Some of the ideas and strategies come from how you were raised. Many come from the experience itself of being a parent. The ideas and strategies also come from powerful workshops you've attended or exceptional books you've read. There are things you want to do to improve your children's self-concepts, to address discipline issues, and to communicate more effectively. Yet what seems so simple when you think, hear, or read about it often turns out to be much more difficult to do. Something gets in the way of transitioning from comprehension to action, from being motivated to actually implementing.
>
> Shifting towards Intentional Self helps you uncover the obstacles, see new patterns, connect the dots in a different way. Shifting towards Intentional Self helps you discover your process for putting these ideas and strategies into practice.

Section 1: The Control Continuum

Irma the PocketCoach's questions and exercises shift you more and more towards Intentional Self. These questions and exercises are what truly enable you to take action and make the changes you want to make. They are the key to understanding how what is being presented fits in, or doesn't fit in, with what you know, believe, and want.

With respect to the Control Continuum, shifting towards Intentional Self gives you the tools to truly understand what you can and can't control. This shift enables you to know what you are **FOCUSING** on and helps you avoid a lot of unnecessary conflict, both internal and external. It allows you to create more room for who your kids are as you make decisions about what they need. And it is this shift that highlights how much power and control you actually do have.

- Describe Intentional Self in your own words.
- What helps you be aware of your beliefs and feelings?
- Identify five things you do on Automatic Pilot.
- What typically happens when you are on Automatic Pilot?
- What are the top three things you try to be and do as a parent?
- What are your top three challenges?

With respect to this workbook:

- What made you choose this book?
- Write down the questions you want answered.
- What will help you slow down long enough to reflect on Irma's questions and complete the exercises?
- How can you get the emotional and pragmatic support you need to follow through?

| A-ha 1:2 |

Meet the Control Continuum

The Illusion of Control ⟵⟶ The Reality of Control

> The Three Components of the Control Continuum Paradigm
> **Our Kids • Us • The Structure We Provide**

Where we stand on the Control Continuum at any given moment is determined by which of these components we FOCUS on controlling. Where we are standing reflects which of these we believe we can and should control and which of these we attempt to control when modifications and adjustments are needed.

To determine where we are standing on this Continuum we must examine our **APES**[2] with respect to control and parenting:

> Our **A**ssumptions, the truths we hold
> Our **P**erspectives, the judgments we make
> Our **E**xpectations, the outcomes we anticipate
> The **S**tories we tell ourselves… the spin we put on things

APES at the Illusion End of the Continuum:

I should be able to *make* my kids do what I want. I can *make* them do what I tell them. I can decide their needs and what's important to them. I am in charge of their choices. I need to change and fix my kids so they grow into healthy, happy, successful adults. For each mistake I make, there are dire consequences. I am solely responsible for ensuring their future success and happiness. If I do everything right, my kids will be fine.

---

[2] APES are copyrighted by Andrea Martin-Pieler and Gail Blohowiak.

Section 1: The Control Continuum

APES at the Reality End of the Continuum

I am not in charge of who my kids are. Taking the word literally, I can't really **make** anyone besides me do anything unless I physically intervene. And as hard as it is to accept, as scary as it is sometimes, I can't always determine what happens to my kids. I can't control who they will grow up to be.

I do, however, have tremendous power and influence. I can choose how I use this power and influence by recognizing which APES and emotions are driving my decisions and actions and by deciding who I will be and the responses I will make. I can provide the structure my kids need to make healthy decisions. By shifting towards Intentional Self, I can select how I want to impact my kids' choices and values. I have to learn who my kids are and what they need. I have to understand what structure is and how to match the structure to the kid-moment. There is so much I can do to maximize the likelihood that my kids will grow into healthy, happy, successful adults.

> **FAQs:** But can't I make my kids do what I want with positive reinforcement and negative consequences?
>
> You can definitely get your kids to do what you want using positive reinforcement and negative consequences. But taking the word literally again, you aren't MAKING your kids do anything. Reinforcement and consequences are part of the **structure**... part of your strategy to influence your kids' behavior and to maximize the likelihood they will do what you want. Your kids can still choose how they will respond to the structure you create.
>
> **Sounds like splitting hairs. What difference does it make what I call it?**
>
> What we call it tends to reflect and affect our APES, what we believe is true and what we FOCUS on. And as you'll discover in Section 2, this has a huge impact on how we approach our kids, how we are received, and how we feel and respond when things don't go the way we want.

> **Our goal must be to shift towards the Reality where we FOCUS on controlling OURSELVES and the STRUCTURE instead of our kids.**
>
> **This is where our true power and influence reside.**

> A-ha 1:3

A Demonstration of the Difference

The Goal: To have your daughter stop swearing at her brother

Scene 1 APES standing in the Illusion: *I can MAKE my daughter stop. I can control her.*

I tell her to stop swearing. If she does, I believe I've controlled her behavior; I have 'made' her stop.

   Reality Note: You have influenced her choice. The choice was still hers to make.

If instead she chooses to continue, I get frustrated that I couldn't MAKE her stop and start yelling. If that doesn't work, in order to have my belief "I can MAKE her stop" become a reality, I put my hand over her mouth. Now, I have indeed MADE her do what I want. She can't move her lips so she stops swearing at her brother immediately.

   Of course, you haven't taught her to stop swearing when your hand isn't there to control her mouth. You haven't given her a reason not to respond by swearing. You have just stopped her from doing it. You haven't helped her see that not doing it pays off. You haven't helped her identify the feelings that lead to the swearing or helped her come up with alternative responses.

   Perhaps you've applied enough pressure that it hurt. Then out of fear of more pain she might not do it again. But the Reality is that without your hand stopping her, it is still her choice whether to swear or not.

Scene 2 APES standing in the Reality: *I can't make her stop unless I physically stop her but there is a lot I can do to influence her choices. I can control myself and provide the structure she needs to help her learn the lessons I want to teach.*

So she swears and I send her to her room for a specified time. I do so calmly and with minimal words. I give her the clear message that swearing at her brother is not acceptable. I stop the behavior by having her leave the situation. I give her space to regroup. I also know she chose to follow my instruction to go to her room. I know the only way I could have MADE her go would have been to carry her.

After the specified time, depending on her age and the frequency of the behavior, we could explore other responses that would be less likely to get her into situations where she might get her clock cleaned. And through openness and acceptance of who she is I help her start to recognize the situations that lead to her swearing at her brother.

By accepting her feelings I create room for her to identify and share them. By making it clear that I don't accept her current behavioral response to those feelings I help her develop alternatives.

Section 1: The Control Continuum

> **A-ha 1:4**

Parents Along the Continuum

As parents, we constantly shift along the continuum in one direction or the other depending on circumstances and which of the three components of the Control Continuum Paradigm we are FOCUSED on controlling.

Stan has four kids between the ages of 6 and 12. Stan feels powerless. His kids don't listen and he believes he should be able to make them. Stan feels that both he and the kids are out-of-control. He states that his kids are running the show whereas, in truth, there's no one running the show. The Reality makes him panic. He *knows* he can't *make* his kids do anything. He lives that every day. The part missing for Stan is the powerful impact he can have if he slowed down long enough to start exploring and adjusting the other two elements he does have control over… his responses and the structure he is providing for his kids.

Janie is a teacher. She believes it's her job to make kids turn out the right way. She's convinced that as long as she holds on to her expectations and standards, kids will respond appropriately. She really cares about kids and provides lots of structure. The majority of kids behave well for her. Yet Janie seems to be constantly frustrated and angry. There are just some kids, growing in numbers she's noticed, who don't behave and won't comply with her rules and directions. She wants to help them but too often finds herself either engaged in battles or giving up. The part missing for Janie is the need to loosen her grip on "this is the right way and this is the wrong way" long enough to see who these other kids are and what they really need from her.

If Janie stopped responding from her anger and frustration and expanded her use of structure, some of her ulcers might heal…

Then there is **Stacy**. Stacy has three teenagers. She finds her daughter Cindy trickier than the other two. Cindy seems to make things so much harder than they need to be. Stacy wishes that things could be easier for this daughter. Stacy knows what works for Stacy. The hard part is that Cindy is not Stacy. Cindy has a different way of moving through life. It took Stacy a while, but eventually she stopped… stopped trying to make Cindy into a mirror image of herself, stopped believing that she had all the answers, and stopped assuming that her way was the best way for Cindy.

Stacy understands the Reality and spends an awful lot of time there. Things aren't exactly what she would wish for Cindy, but she sees all of her daughter's vulnerabilities and strengths. Stacy has made herself available to the lessons Cindy has for her about the mom Cindy needs her to be.

And Cindy, in her own way and according to her own time frame, has learned to incorporate much of her mom's wisdom and approach into her own style and worldview.

Aim Your Control, Control Your Aim.

The Illusion of Control   **The Reality of Control**

> **From where you are standing right now:**
> - I know I can control…
> - I wish I could control…
> - I have my greatest influence when I…
>
> ———◊———
>
> **Describe the Illusion and the Reality in your own words.**
>
> **What are you unsure of?**
>
> **What do you disagree with?**
>
> **Which part of all this feels right?**

Notes

> There is a difference between being in control
> and trying to control our kids.

Section 2

Kids and Control

What we attend to tells our kids what's important to us.

Section 2: Kids and Control

Understanding the Impact

A Story[3]

Sarah and Katie were engaged in a raging sibling battle. After about ten minutes they were both ready to walk out the door with their intense anger hanging in the air. I told them they couldn't leave it that way. They stayed and worked things out.

Sarah called later and said: "Mom, you're amazing. You have so much control over us. We both just wanted to leave but we didn't. Even at 20 and 23-years-old neither of us would have left the house when you told us not to."

The word control threw me. I don't see myself as having control over them. I have always known that I had tremendous influence with respect to who they are and the choices they make, but NOT CONTROL!

So the next day I asked Sarah and Katie about it...

Sarah's take on it:

"The reason I stayed was because you and Katie mean more to me than my pride. As angry as I was at Katie, I could never leave the situation because I knew how much it would really hurt her and you. I love you guys way too much to ever let my anger be prolonged. I think we all know better than to leave mad at someone."

Katie's take on it:

Comparing my "control" to that of Lisa, her friend Brandy's mom:

"I hate the control that Lisa has over Brandy. It's like Lisa is always trying to get inside Brandy's head and take over rather than letting Brandy make up her own mind. Your control is good because it still lets us decide who we want to be and where we want to go in this world. I don't think Lisa believes that Brandy can do much without her help. You on the other hand believe that Sarah and I can do anything. Sure you help us out with a lot of things but you've taught us how capable we are at doing things on our own."

---

[3] Sarah and Katie stories are shared with their permission.

Section 2: Kids and Control

When we parent from the Reality our kids:

- ➢ Do a great job recognizing what's important and making their decisions accordingly.
- ➢ Don't feel like we are trying to 'get inside their heads and take over'.

In this section we will explore in detail what happens when we parent from the extreme ends of the Control Continuum.

Our Focus

The Illusion	The Reality
Controlling our kids' choices and decisions	Controlling ourselves through practiced awareness as we teach, guide, and influence our kids' choices and decisions
Fixing and changing our kids	Seeing and understanding our kids to know what really needs fixing and changing and what doesn't
A guaranteed future of happiness and success for our kids'	An understanding of how to manage structure to increase the likelihood of our kids' future happiness and success

Aim Your Control, Control Your Aim.

A-ha 2:1

Obstacles and Fallacies at the Illusion End

**I. Kids are born to struggle for independence.
Standing in the Illusion we are battling Mother Nature.**

Starting well before we are usually ready, kids begin struggling for independence and control. This struggle varies from kid to kid and within the same kid. Every parent can attest to the fact that this struggle involves an infinite range of intensity and finesse.

This struggle can be excruciating. Yet when we are not caught in the throes of some crisis, we know this struggle means all is well. We are reminded of this each time we see the alternative, the kid who doesn't strive for independence or the adult who never did.

And the more difficulty our kids are having understanding and managing their own feelings and choices, the more the Illusion interferes with their growth and development. They may just give up. They may allow us to manage and be in charge of their feelings, their choices, and their lives.

Or they may become less and less tolerant and more resistant as they feel backed into a corner. And the more we believe we can control their preferences and choices, the more we add fuel to the fire and the more intense the 'bust loose syndrome' becomes. For the more controlled kids feel, the more challenging they may become and the harder they may rebel. As a result, they may be less able to establish an independent self in a healthy, positive way.

On the other hand, the more in control kids feel, within the limits and support of **Purposeful Structure** (Ways we intentionally modify the environment within which our kids live- Section 5), the less there is for them to fight against!

Example

I clearly remember the first time Sarah opened the refrigerator door without asking. She was 2-years-old at the time. It shocked me that she did that. Then it shocked me that I was so shocked. Up until that point I had no idea that my need to control her actions was so strong. Thank goodness it happened when she was 2-years-old!

We can't choose the Path of Independence our kids take, but we can have great influence over how much of a struggle it is, both for them and for ourselves.

Section 2: Kids and Control

- What do you remember about being a kid struggling for control?
- What helped you?
- What made it harder?
- How does this tie in with what you are learning about the Illusion and the Reality?
- When does your kids' struggle for independence feel right?
- When does it seem too hard for them? For you?
- How does this tie in with what you are learning about the Illusion and the Reality?

II. Kids who feel strong and capable make healthier decisions. Standing in the Illusion we are sabotaging our own efforts.

When our main concern is changing and fixing our kids we tend to focus on what's wrong rather than on what's right. We are much more likely to undermine our kids' belief in themselves and much more likely to feed into confusion and self-doubt.

For some kids this might not be too detrimental. As with most things, it's a continuum and a range. Depending on the kid, they might do well in spite of this. Depending on the circumstances, they might stay strong and confident.

However, the more challenging your kids' behaviors are for you the more your kids are at a disadvantage. Because the more challenging their behaviors are the more likely you have been telling them all the things they are NOT…

When we overwhelm our kids with messages they need fixing we interfere with their getting a clear understanding of who they really are. We make it harder for them to shift towards Intentional Self and realize their full potential.

- What adds to your self-confidence?
- How do you add to your kids' self-confidence?

18

III. We want our kids to accept responsibility.
Standing in the Illusion we are missing the boat.

People accept responsibility for what they believe they are in charge of and what they feel they can control. And the more responsible people feel for who they are and what they do, the more they believe in their ability to determine what happens to them. The less out-of-control they feel.

When our kids accept responsibility they make healthier choices. They don't see themselves as victims of society, of adults, or of their own impulses.

The kids who do see themselves as victims are the ones who don't even try because 'it won't make a difference anyway.'

When we stand in the Illusion, we believe we are in charge of our kids' decisions, we think we should be able to control every choice they make.

**When we are standing in the Illusion
we absolve our kids of their responsibilities
because we've made those responsibilities our own!**

A Story

I made Katie a doctor's appointment two weeks ahead of time. She likes to know when I schedule things for her so she can plan accordingly. I told her when the appointment was. She acknowledged it but didn't write it down.

I could have continued reminding her about it over the next two weeks so she wouldn't be surprised the day of the appointment. Or I could have let it go, knowing my next involvement would be the day of the appointment when, given who I know she is, she would get herself there.

Standing in the Illusion, I would have felt compelled to make sure she was not surprised at the last minute. I would have made it my mission to protect her from something unpleasant. Standing in the Reality, I recognize what I am responsible for, what she's responsible for, and I have more choices about what might be best for her and for me, both in the short-term and the long-term…

Section 2: Kids and Control

- What do you feel responsible for as a parent?
- What do you hold your kids responsible for?
- What would your kids say they are responsible for?
- What's the hardest thing about deciding who's responsible for what?
- What makes this decision easier for you?

IV. We don't want to OVERREACT or LIMIT OUR OPTIONS when things go 'wrong'. Standing in the Illusion we are setting ourselves up.

When our kids make decisions that could impact their health, safety, and happiness, we need to perform a delicate balancing act. We need to weigh what we believe/know is good for our kids with what they believe is good for them. We need to address their ineffective choices or actions without condemning their overall decision-making process and without making them shut down or pull away.

Standing in the Illusion we are much more likely to respond nonproductively. We are much more likely to get pulled towards Automatic Pilot as we experience not only fear or anger regarding their choices but also disappointment and frustration with ourselves for not DOING OUR JOB. We were supposed to be able to control and prevent those unhealthy, unsafe, ineffective choices and behaviors!

Standing in the Illusion when things go wrong, we have not met our own expectations and we feel less in control of ourselves. We are much more likely to react from intense fear and anger and much less able to make choices that help the situation. So things escalate, we get even more frustrated, angry or afraid, and two things tend to happen.

First, our tone, choice of words, and actions reflect our frustration, anger, and fear. As a result, our kids are more likely to shut down, clam up, or pull away.

And second, we are unable see the broad spectrum of intervention options available to us.

Aim Your Control, Control Your Aim.

When our frustration, anger, or fear have control over us we are more likely to rely on negative consequences or punishment 'to get that darn kid back under control.'

What else can I take away from her? He can't do that to me.
What can I do to him to make him sorry?

If this is our response all the time, instead of sending the message, "You are responsible for your choices and behavior", we might actually be encouraging our kids to blame us.

This <negative consequence> happened to me because dad is angry.
I didn't do anything. He's being wacko again.

And when we are standing in the Illusion on Automatic Pilot there's a good chance the kids are right. Maybe we are just being wacko again!

- Describe three circumstances where you were able to step back and choose how to respond.
- Describe three circumstances where you regret having reacted angrily or from your fears.
- How do these examples tie into what you know about the Control Continuum?

V. We don't have all the answers.
Standing in the Illusion we are more likely to believe that we do.

When we feel responsible for ensuring our kids' futures, we are much less likely to try and understand what they are experiencing. We tend not to be open and curious about who they are. We don't listen very well. After all, why should we listen when we already have it all figured out!

When we think we have all the answers our APES go unnoticed and unquestioned. We turn our assumptions and generalizations into **FACTS**.

We let our judgments interfere with hearing the real message or hanging in long enough with our kids to help them uncover it.

When we think we have all the answers our APES get in the way and it's hard to get past what we believe to be true. We get stuck in our own stories about who our kids are or what they are doing.

He's just trying to make me mad.
She's just being lazy.

Section 2: Kids and Control

When we assume we have all the answers we stop looking for all those answers our kids have for us. And we miss teaching many of the lessons our kids need to learn because we haven't discovered what those lessons are.

- What do you know for sure about each of your kids?
- What makes you so certain?
- Would your kids agree with you?
- When do your assumptions and expectations make it difficult to hear what your kids are trying to tell you?
- How uncomfortable are you with the thought of not having all the answers?

VI. We perpetuate Self-Defeating Cycles.
Standing in the Illusion we are unable to slow down and step back.

Our kids try to assert their independence and their control in what turn out to be unsuccessful ways or ways for which we aren't prepared. They make what we consider poor choices. They behave unsafely or ineffectively or in ways we simply don't like. We get afraid, angry, and frustrated. We increase our attempts to control their choices and take away more of their control and independence. They fight that tooth and nail. We get more frustrated, angry, and afraid and increase our attempts to control them. They fight harder for control. We fight harder for control.

And this cycle can start anywhere with kids of any age.

… With the 2-year-old: "I don't think you should pour orange juice on your cereal."
… With the 15-year-old: "Sure I love you, but you're still too young to date."
… With the 21-year-old: "But you can't afford your own apartment."

When we're not standing in the Illusion we can have powerful influence by staying centered in who we want to be, providing the structure appropriate for our kids' ages and abilities, and helping our kids feel seen, heard, and acknowledged. We might not always get the outcomes we want. There are no guarantees regardless of where we are standing. But when we are not in the Illusion we are much more likely to respond in ways that maximize the likelihood that what comes to pass will be what's best for our kids.

Aim Your Control, Control Your Aim.

- What happens when your kids don't do something you thought you could MAKE them do?
- Describe a typical Self-defeating cycle with your kids.

When we stop trying to <u>make</u> our kids change, it's amazing to see the changes they're willing to make!

FAQ: Don't I need to control my kids when they seem really out-of-control, headed for disaster?

When kids are really out-of-control we have to be our calmest to prevent further escalation. We remain calmest when we are objective and making decisions with a clear head, when we are not being blind-sided by our own strong emotions. By standing in the Reality, we feel in charge and are better able to identify and consider several options. We are able to make choices rather than reacting impulsively from Automatic Pilot.

We could 'control' our kids by containing them physically, by locking them in their rooms for instance.

A Reality Note: If there is no lock on the door, what we would be doing is providing Purposeful Structure rather than 'controlling' them. They would still have a choice about whether to stay in the room.

And isn't that the scary part? Not having the lock on the door when we feel our kids are out-of-control. The fact is, the more we parent from the Reality of Control, the more likely it is that our kids will choose to comply with our rules, our structure, and stay in the room.

Section 2: Kids and Control

A-ha 2:2

The Beauty of the Reality

"You cannot control the wind, but you can adjust your sails."
- Anthony Robbins -

I. When we shift towards the Reality our kids feel powerful and develop a strong sense of ownership for their choices.

Our kids are much more likely to learn cause and effect. Through our demeanor, support, and the structure we provide, they learn that this choice or behavior results in this outcome. And they feel powerful.

*Hey, by changing my behavior or attitude I can change what happens.
There is a whole lot I can do to affect the responses I get
from my mom, my teachers, and my friends.*

Our kids internalize responsibility for their choices and for who they are.

When we stand in the Reality, our actions, words, and interventions empower our kids by giving them the message, "You CAN make a difference".

> **And empowered kids make more successful choices everywhere they go, no matter who they are with.**

- Describe a situation where one of your kids amazed you by demonstrating ownership for what she/he was doing, the choices she/he was making.
- What were you doing as this situation took place?
- What weren't you doing?

II. When we shift towards the Reality we are far less likely to overreact on Automatic Pilot.

In the Reality, when our kids make choices we don't agree with:
- We are able to remain more objective.
- We can step back and view their choices as an indication that more learning/growth needs to occur and/or that more or different structure is needed.
- We clearly communicate our expectations and give feedback.
- We are more confident that we can help them.
- We know our responsibility lies in making/choosing our own thoughtful responses.
- We have different ways to intervene so we don't rely solely on negative consequences or punishment.
- We feel in control and increase the likelihood of effectively helping our kids.

**Standing in the Reality coming from Intentional Self
we are better able to tap into our wisdom
and gain confidence in our decisions.**

- Think of a time your child made a choice you didn't agree with.
- Were you pleased with your response or your reaction?
- How does this fit in with what you know about the Control Continuum and Automatic Pilot?

Section 2: Kids and Control

III. When we shift towards the Reality our decisions and actions transmit the 'right' messages.

When we stand in the Reality of Control we are much more likely to send messages like these to our kids:

You have lots of answers... You are able to make great things happen...
Your feelings and beliefs are important to me... You deserve consideration and respect...
You are worth knowing... You are not alone....

As we make decisions about rules and consequences (about structure), we are able to weigh the *short term gain* of our interventions and responses against the *longer term impact*. We are able to consistently ask ourselves, *Will my choice or action send the 'right' message?*

Sending the 'right' messages engages our kids. Sending the 'right' messages helps them develop ownership in their own growth, happiness, and success.

**When our kids hear the 'right' messages
they are much more receptive to what the world has to offer.
And they are much more aware of what they have to give back.**

Isn't that what we want for our kids?

- What strengths do your kids have to share with the world?
- What messages do you send to help them recognize these strengths?
- What specifically do you do and say that sends these messages?

26

IV. When we shift towards the Reality we truly come to know our kids and what they need from us.

Standing in the Reality helps us create the space where

- ➢ We are more available to pay attention because we are not being blinded by unconscious APES and unrecognized emotions.
- ➢ Our kids are not hiding from us as much either intentionally or unintentionally.

We are better able to see their strengths, their hot buttons, and their fears. We come to understand what they really care about, what they worry about, and what they are proud of. We come to know their APES and how those impact their choices and actions.

As we shift towards the Reality our kids teach us:

- What they are confused about
- Where they need help setting priorities
- How they have learned to get their needs met
- Where they are locked into self-defeating APES
- What interferes with their understanding
- How they process information and make sense of their world

And as a result we can teach our kids the lessons they need to learn.

- What are your kids confused about?
- What are your kids proud of?
- What's most important to your kids right now?
- What would they really like you to know about them?

Section 2: Kids and Control

V. When we shift towards the Reality we become a mirror for our kids. For as they share with us they come to see themselves more clearly.

When we stand in the Reality our kids are more willing and able to let us help them explore who they are. As we question and clarify in the spirit of love and curiosity (versus judgment and blame), they gain insight into their perspectives and feelings. Standing in the Reality we facilitate their shift towards Intentional Self.

Our kids discover how their APES impact their feelings and affect their choices and actions. They develop a deeper understanding of how to CHOOSE their place in the family and in the world.

They begin to assess who they are and who they want to be. And just as they come to identify and value their own strengths, they become familiar with the choices and behaviors that are unsuccessful. They identify those behaviors that need adjustment. They develop ownership in the change process because they are part of it.

When we stand in the Reality we empower our kids to determine what path they will take as they move out into their world fully armed with our knowledge, wisdom, and love.

> **In essence, when we stand in the Reality our kids learn how to write their own scripts with us as their trusted co-authors.**

- When interacting with you, what do your kids see reflected back about them?
- How does this help them make choices?
- When interacting with your kids, what do you see reflected back about you?
- How does this help you make choices?
- For each of your children, describe how you are most effective helping them learn about themselves.

A-ha 2:3

A Bottom Line...
Our Kids Get Really Scared

There are times when they have all the answers and times when they feel they don't know anything. Times when they catch a glimpse of the adult world and can't wait to get there. And there are times when they don't want to go anywhere near it. It's so hard to keep up with. It is so easy for us to get lost.

We must pay close attention to ourselves and to them. When we are standing in the Illusion we are much more likely to be on Automatic Pilot and miss a whole lot.

Our kids need help navigating the choppy waters of growing up. But we can't do it from the outside or all on our own terms. It is their process and they get to choose how much they will ALLOW us to help.

And they won't let us help as long as we keep pounding them with everything that's wrong and as long as we assume we have all the answers. They won't let us help as long as they have to struggle with us for their very identities.

When we stand in the Reality and stop focusing on controlling and fixing them, our kids are more likely to:

➢ Loosen their death-grip on the struggle for independence
➢ Worry less about being misunderstood and found lacking
➢ Let down their guard and stop protecting themselves
➢ Trust our words and actions

When we stand in the Reality our kids are much more likely to let us in.

- What do you assume your kids are afraid of?
- What makes you think so?
- When your kids share their feelings, how do you show that you are listening?
- When do you feel compelled to fix and solve?

Section 2: Kids and Control

> A-ha 2:4

Okay, An Admission
Controlling kids gets quicker results

We must remember, however, the only real way to control our kids and **make** them do something, is by physically moving or containing them.

And when we do this the change is immediate. That's why this is an attractive option when safety is a factor. If two kids are physically fighting, someone steps in to break it up. When a toddler is about to walk in front of a moving car, mom or dad will grab the kid.

Short of physical intervention, however, there is no way to guarantee control over another person.

BUT, there are ways to make kids BELIEVE we have ultimate control over them.

In the extreme, we can do this with actual or implied threat of harm. We can demoralize kids and break their spirits. We can contribute to their feelings of being powerless victims.

These can be awfully convincing. And of course we all know they come at a huge cost.

So at this point you might be thinking, *I have never... I would never...* But we all need to be aware of the possibilities because these techniques occur on a lot of levels and along vast continuums with respect to intention and intensity.

When we are standing towards the Illusion end on Automatic Pilot there is a greater likelihood that some of these harmful methods may subtly slip into our repertoire.

"We are all capable of doing things that may demoralize our kids and contribute to their feeling powerless."

- What's your reaction to this statement?

Being aware of this reaction may increase your openness to the possibilities explored on the next few pages in **A-ha 2:5**.

| A-ha 2:5 |

Several Suspicious Characters

The following characters highlight how seemingly straight forward actions may in fact be more complicated. They are not meant as rigid examples of right/wrong behavior or pure/evil intention. Reflecting on these characters is another way to turn off the Automatic Pilot switch. Familiarizing ourselves with them allows us to stand more solidly in the Reality and understand some of the repetitive feedback we might be getting from our kids.

Our kids sometimes get annoyed with us 'just because'. And sometimes our kids get annoyed with us 'just because' we are being annoying!

This often has to do with how controlling our kids perceive us to be.

Helpful Hannah

We all know who she is. She's the one always doing things for her kids. Hannah is so good at observing and anticipating that she knows what her kids need even before they know it.

A Story

I was able to read 15-year-old Peter so well. I could see when he didn't understand something. I could tell when he had a question. I knew when he was getting frustrated. And I would approach him before he had a chance to ask for help or before he could decide if he wanted to ask. I offered my help before he had a chance to try and figure things out on his own. After about one month in my class Peter stopped accepting my help. Instead, he would get angry with me and refuse all assistance.

It took me a while but I finally realized that in my mission to help I wasn't respecting Peter's individuality. I wasn't letting him learn to recognize his own feelings and reactions. I wasn't allowing him any control of who he was, what he was doing, or how he was going to ask for help. In short, I was driving Peter crazy!

Possible messages Helpful Hannah sends:

You need me for everything. You can't do without me. I know you better than you know yourself. You don't have to worry about anything because I will take care of it all. I can protect you from hurting or wanting. You don't know how to do anything. I don't trust you to take care of your own needs.

Section 2: Kids and Control

… Choosing our kids' clothes, checking their homework, stepping in to resolve every sibling argument, refilling the glass of milk before Susie even downs that last drop…

All of these could simply reflect our desire to help. And they could be an extension of our need to feel useful or to control and have it our own way. They could be something our kids want. And they could be examples of us not recognizing when we have gone overboard or when our kids' requirements have changed.

Helping is complicated because there are so many factors involved:

- Our intentions and needs
- Whether or not our kids really require the help
- Our kids' struggle for independence and how willing they are to accept our help.

Standing in the Reality and coming from Intentional Self enables us to know our kids. And the better we know our kids the more we can 'read' what's going on and successfully choose when and how to help.

Dear Abby

Pick a topic, any topic, and she has advice. Abby is not able to keep her mouth shut. If she has an opinion, a suggestion, or a 'better way', she'll apprise you of it.

As with her cousin Hannah, Abby tends to carve out a huge presence in her kids' lives and may send many of the same messages.

- When do you turn into Hannah or Abby?
- Describe a scenario in which your kids resented Hannah or Abby showing up.
- What could you have done instead?

Director Dan

No matter what task is at hand he'll tell his kids exactly how to do it, step by step by step. And then he'll probably repeat each step ten times just to make sure they got it.

"Do your homework as soon as you get home from school, sit in the den, be sure to turn the light on and the TV off, have your snack at 4:23 and don't forget to wash the dishes. Did you hear me? I said do your homework as soon as you get home from school, sit in the den, be sure to turn the light on…"

Dan may be coming completely from Intentional Self as he stands in the Reality providing Purposeful Structure. Or he may be underestimating his kids or operating on Automatic Pilot.

Example

I upset my kids whenever catching a flight is involved. I flip to Automatic Pilot, I shift to the Illusion, and I become Director Dan personified. As if my kids don't know enough to zip the suitcase shut before picking it up. Oh brother…

- When does Dan take over your personality? (Suggestion: Ask your kids.)
- What messages does Director Dan send kids?

Narrator Nick

As he watches his son jog to home plate, Nick yells out, "Yo, you're up". For Nick, seeing what his kids are doing triggers his thoughts, statements, and questions. His kids are already in action and basically Nick is describing the action. He gets back a lot of, "Dad, can't you see I'm already doing that".

Example

I observe Katie getting ready to look in her overnight bag and say, "Do you want to check and make sure you have everything you need?" Or I watch as Sarah reaches for the plates and ask her if she would mind setting the table.

Section 2: Kids and Control

Nick is great at including himself in the action, playing a bigger role than he might otherwise if he were to stop narrating...

- Is there a Narrator Nick in your life?
- How does Nick make you feel?
- Watch for those times when you narrate.

Peter Positive

"You're such a good, quiet little girl."

Our kids need and deserve positive feedback. One of the ways we show them what is important to us is by attending to behaviors that we value and acknowledging them when we see them. Positive feedback and attention are one of the backbones of Purposeful Structure. The caution here is not to forget to acknowledge who our kids are and not just who we want them to be. We must not ignore what's important to them.

So Peter may be providing effective structure or he may be trying to turn his kids into something they aren't. It's helpful for Peter to step back and observe what he's doing.

- What do you notice and reinforce in your kids?
- What do they wish you would notice and reinforce?

Christine the Critic

"You missed this spot, and this one and this one. Oh my, and this one over here too."

Negative feedback is also part of Purposeful Structure. It is one way to teach and prompt kids. Christine takes it to such an extreme however, that nothing her kids do is ever right or good enough.

Christine might do well to notice what this tendency is doing to her kids. Sticking this closely to our own agendas takes a toll on our kids and impacts their relationship with us and the rest of their world.

- How do you know when you are facing a problem that needs addressing versus something that is just different from what you want or expect?
- When are you most likely to be 'picking at' rather than teaching?

Fuzzy Fred

He's not very clear or forthcoming with his requirements so he says things like, "You can come out of your room when I feel you are ready".

Blurring our expectations and sending mixed messages makes it hard for our kids to know where they stand. By doing this we are the only ones able to assess the outcomes. We are in complete control as our kids just have to continue guessing. We are making up the rules and keeping the rule book a secret.

- When is Fuzzy Fred most likely to show up?
- How does it feel when he captures your voice?
- What do your kids do?
- What helps you communicate your expectations more clearly?

Section 2: Kids and Control

Which Suspicious Characters do you need to be on the lookout for?
(Give 'em a face...)

| MOST WANTED | MOST WANTED | MOST WANTED |

Write down what you intend to do about them.

**What other characters are lurking within?
Write their descriptions...**

> A-ha 2:6

Another Bottom Line...
No Need to be Perfect

We help and advise because we love our kids... and sometimes we help and advise because we want to be needed and because we want to know we still have a role to play in our kids' lives.

We give instructions because we want things to turn out well for our kids... and sometimes we give instructions because our way is the RIGHT way, the ONLY way.

We give our kids positive feedback because we want them to see their own strengths... and sometimes we give this feedback to turn our kids into us or into the anti-us depending on how we feel about ourselves and particular traits we have.

We give our kids negative feedback because we want them to avoid trouble and problems... and sometimes we give negative feedback because we are angry or stressed out.

We have to let all of this be okay. The more we can accept all of who we are the more room we create for all of who our kids are. And the more we can be the parents we want to be, the parents our kids need us to be.

Accepting ourselves doesn't mean not caring or not doing the best we can. It means knowing that when we are less than perfect, which we will be **A LOT**, we don't sink into despair or guilt. Because it does all start with us....

Section 2: Kids and Control

If we beat ourselves up for being less than perfect, we are far more likely to get extreme and shift towards the '*too*', with our kids:

Either by being TOO harsh: Not allowing them to make mistakes because we want 'more for them' or because we never learned to tolerate 'less than perfect'.

Or by being TOO lax: Bending over so far backwards that we don't provide the limits and structure they need because we don't want them to feel the way we do.

By accepting that we don't need to be perfect we can allow our kids to not be perfect.

And that's what helps them learn from their mistakes rather than ignoring them or falling apart when they make them.

- Which Characters had you chuckling in self-recognition?
- Which ones are hardest to accept in yourself?
- Which ones make you feel sad?
- Which ones make you feel guilty?
- What will help you let go of the guilt while you work on minimizing the Characters' negative impact on your kids?

Aim Your Control, Control Your Aim.

Kids and Control Check-In

1. I know I can control…

2. I wish I could control…

3. I have my greatest influence when I…

4. I help my kids feel in control by…

5. I can do more of that by…

6. I send the 'wrong' messages when I…

7. In order to stop doing this I need to…

8. I encourage my kids to share by…

9. I notice where I'm standing when I remember…

10. What I 'buy' about the Control Continuum is…

11. The parts I don't accept are…

12. What I believe instead is…

Notes

The more powerless people feel the less responsible they feel.

Section 3

In Charge of Me

We absolutely can create
a space of wisdom,
understanding,
and support
that our kids willingly
turn towards
and continue to
return to

THROUGHOUT THEIR LIVES.

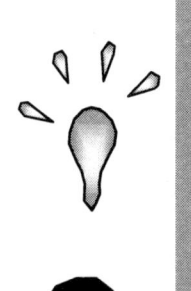

Section 3: In Charge of Me

Exploring Barriers, Expanding Perspectives

Section I introduced the three components of the Control Continuum Paradigm: Us, Our Kids, and Structure. We shift towards the Reality of Control when we:

- Stop focusing on controlling our kids.

- Realize the incredible impact we have as we provide structure and manage those parts of the environment that are within our control.

- Increase our self awareness by turning off the Automatic Pilot in order to choose what we will say and do. Having our words, actions, and decisions based on understanding and love and rather than unconscious reactions to fear and anger.

In this section, you'll explore potential barriers that may be encountered along the way and engage in exercises to enhance your ability to overcome them. The A-ha's in this section will help you choose and use the concepts, tools, and strategies in Sections 4, 5, and 6.

Work with Irma. The broader your perspective and the more prepared you are to face uncertainty and fear the more open you can be to learning additional ways to interact with your kids.

Section 3: In Charge of Me

A-ha 3:1

What Makes Shifting So Hard?

What makes shifting towards the Reality so difficult? Why do we believe our job is to control our kids, MAKE them change? Why do we sometimes act as if our kids are broken and our job is to fix them?

A. It could be a general belief we hold about people.

One of our unnoticed APES might be that we can indeed *make* other people do what we want, that we can control the choices our spouses, our friends, our co-workers make.

B. It could be we think it is somehow different when it comes to our kids.

We know we can't control the other people in our lives. We know we can't re-make our partners and friends according to our blueprints, no matter how great the plan or honorable the intention. Yet when it comes to our kids, especially when they behave in challenging ways or make ineffective choices, we get all nutty. We come to believe our job IS to revise them and control who they are….

- What evidence do you have that you can control other people?
- What shows you this is untrue?
- When has this belief interfered with a non-parent relationship?
- Who seems to be trying to control you?
- How do you respond to this person?
- Identify three unintended results you get when you try to fix and control your kids.

Aim Your Control, Control Your Aim.

C. It could be we are feeling out-of-control.

We know we can't make other people do anything. We know we can't control them. But when things get busy and hectic and we start feeling out-of-control we slip into ineffective patterns. We start grabbing at anything that might make us feel less off kilter, anything to help us organize our world and reintroduce some predictability.

- How do you know when you are out-of-control?
- What does it feel like?
- What do you typically do when you feel out-of-control?

(Refer to **Strategy 25 Aim your control… Control your aim**, Section 4.)

D. It could be we don't realize what we truly can control.

We think controlling our kids is THE WAY to take care of them. This is the only way to be a GOOD PARENT. We don't understand the other possibilities that exist.

- How did you define GOOD PARENT before you began reading this book?
- What do you now believe are the characteristics of a GOOD PARENT?
- If your definition of GOOD PARENT has changed, what made the difference?
- What have you started doing that reflects your new definition?
- What have you stopped doing that reflects your new definition?

Section 3: In Charge of Me

E. And it could be FEAR

We so often start grasping for control of the wrong things when we feel afraid. As parents we may have these fears:

- **Fear #1:** **What if** my kids grow up to be failures, criminals, or unhappy?

- **Fear #2:** **What if** I don't control my kids and they can't control themselves?

- **Fear #3:** **What if** I look like a push-over or set a bad precedent?

- **Fear #4:** **What if** my kids get real good at using manipulation to get their own way?

- **Fear #5:** **What if** my kids WIN and learn the wrong lessons in the process?

Exercise 3:1

1. For each fear:
    a. Is this one of your fears?
    b. If so, describe the circumstances when you experience this fear.
    c. How might you alleviate this fear?

   (Refer to **A-ha 3:8 Those Pesky WhatIfs**, this section)

2. Reflect in writing on the following questions:
    a. What are you most afraid of as a parent?
    b. How can you tell when your decisions are based on fear?
    c. What would you do differently if you weren't afraid?
    d. How are your fears helpful?

Shifting towards Intentional Self involves facing the fear to get past the fear.

Aim Your Control, Control Your Aim.

> A-ha 3:2

My Catch 22

So we understand the Reality and can operate at that end of the Control Continuum most of the time. We know how to slow down, step back, and observe our APES and our interactions with our kids. We've gotten really good at knowing what we are responsible for and what our kids are responsible for. We are learning how to let our kids make choices and to be there for them as they need us. We are so good we can even respect our kids' right to make lousy choices.

Except under certain circumstances…

Times when, no matter how much we understand and believe in the Reality, it is extremely hard to step back in order to determine what would truly be in our kids' best interest. Those are the **Catch 22s**, situations we find ourselves in that pull us back towards the Illusion.

How does recognizing our Catch 22s help?

When we understand our personal Catch 22s:

- We can be better prepared when they pop up and not be caught so off-guard that we automatically turn towards the Illusion…

- We might be able to do some prevention work in order to cross them off our **Catch 22** list…

- We are better able to determine whether or not to get actively involved in our kids' decision-making process. And when we do choose to get involved we are more capable of doing so from the Reality.

Circumstances with the strongest **Catch 22**, the ones we are most likely to grab for control of all the wrong things, are the very circumstances where it is essential that we stand firmly in the Reality.

A Story

Talk about big, long term impact… When Katie was diagnosed with diabetes I lost control of me and tried to replace it by controlling her. I constantly watched over and questioned her as she ate and checked her sugar levels. I nagged and advised. I begged her to talk to me about her feelings. Out of extreme fear I forgot how capable she was. I forgot what she needed from me especially at such a devastating time. At a time when so much of her life all of a sudden felt like it was beyond her control.

What a disservice I was doing by trying to usurp the control she did have…

Section 3: In Charge of Me

Here are some variables that influence the magnitude of our **Catch 22s** and some actions we might take to lessen their impact and remain in the Reality:

A. How public (and embarrassing) our child's choice is:

You are in the grocery store and your 5-year-old is having a full blown temper-tantrum or your 16-year-old shows up at the family reunion wearing enough make-up to put Bozo to shame…

- Know ahead of time what is open to negotiation and what is not
- Engage your kids in some pre-planning (Refer to **Strategy 16 Co-design**, Section 4)
- Have a back-up plan that includes your options
- Maintain your sense of humor
- Keep your eye on the big picture
- Be prepared to leave the situation

B. How big and long term the impact of the choice might be:

Your second semester senior in college announces, "I'm dropping out of school and joining the circus"… Your 12-year-old insists, "But Joe's my friend. He didn't know the car was stolen."

- Slow down and clarify where you do have control
- Tell your child how she/he can help you feel more comfortable

C. How fragile, vulnerable we feel:

You've been up all night… You just lost your job… The puppy missed the paper again… You need something to be going right…

- Take an inventory of what is bothering you so you know what isn't bothering you

D. How much of a time crunch we are experiencing:

The school play starts in twenty minutes and your 10-year-old can't decide what shoes to wear…

- Start earlier
- Give short, specific instructions
- Prepare kids for transitions
- Engage your kids in pre-planning (Refer to **Strategy 16 Co-design**, Section 4)

Aim Your Control, Control Your Aim.

E. How well behaved other people's children appear:

At play group, all the other kids are sharing so nicely and your son is hitting anyone who comes within five feet of his truck…

- Take a breath and remember what you know about kids in general and about your own kids in particular
- Take a step back to find some humor in the situation
- Know how to adjust the structure to meet your kid's needs

F. How much we are exposed to other people's fears:

Your friend says to you, "I don't trust my daughter; I think she's doing drugs." Or the neighborhood newspaper reports on the epidemic of cheating on final exams.

- Talk to your kids (Refer to **Strategy 3 Put it on the table**, Section 4)
- Stay grounded in what you know about your kids and go from there

G. How high our expectations are:

You go on your first family vacation in five years. You are looking so forward to getting away from MTV and spending quality time with your kids. And your teenagers won't stop complaining about how bored they are.

- Recognize how high your expectations really are
- Consider what is possible even if your expectations aren't fully met

Exercise 3:2

1. List your **Catch 22s**.
2. When are they most likely to show up?
3. When have you successfully kept them from catching you off-guard?
4. Describe a time they completely blind-sided you.
5. Identify how you could have been better prepared for them.

Section 3: In Charge of Me

> A-ha 3:3

Paying Attention
Awareness of what's going on both within us and around us.

Paying attention is a prerequisite for everything else we are trying to do:
- Identifying what we are focused on controlling at any given moment
- Noticing what's working and what's not
- Seeing our kids and understanding what they need from us
- Recognizing when changing circumstances call for different responses from us

And by the way, it is slowing down enough to pay attention that allows us to live full, rich lives so we don't wake up one day wondering where it all went and where we were as our kids grew up…

Paying attention is both a **prerequisite** for, and a **product** of, shifting towards Intentional Self.

Paying attention takes conscious practice. And the more we practice the better we get at it. Plus it's easy to practice because we can practice anywhere, anytime, with anything…

Some ways to practice:

- No matter where you are, choose to shift your focus between what you see, what you hear, and what you smell.
- While exercising, attend to the muscle that is being worked.
- When you are eating, turn off the TV, stop reading, and notice what swallowing does to your Adams Apple.
  (While you're at it choose to taste the food.)
- When your kids are talking to you notice where your attention is and practice bringing it back to their eyes.
- Sit quietly and observe what comes up. Without really trying, notice the difference between thoughts you are thinking, emotions you are experiencing, and physical sensations you are feeling.
- See a flame change colors.
- Hear what silence sounds like.
- Working at your computer, see your fingers.
  (Only for people like me who never learned to type the 'right' way)
- Put up a sign at work or at home that says "Mindfulness" or "NOW" and notice it three times a day.

Aim Your Control, Control Your Aim.

- Decide that each time you see your children you will remember to come back to what they are saying or what their faces are expressing.

- Carry something in your pocket that, when you touch it, will remind you to pay attention.

- Decide every hour on the hour you are going to check into the NOW.
  (Set the timer on your watch.)

- Carve out a few minutes each day to meditate.
  (And really do it.)

- When something sad happens, check out what sad feels like.

- When something good happens, remember to notice and be grateful.

Exercise 3:3

1. Choose two ways to practice Paying Attention. Choose from either the above list or make up your own. Do them for a week.

2. Keep a log of what you notice and what you learn.

3. Keep choosing different strategies and see which ones work best for you.

(Hint: In order to know what works for you, you have to be paying attention to what you are trying to do!)

Section 3: In Charge of Me

> **A-ha 3:4**

Either-Or

Either-Or is a category of Great APES we use to interpret and give meaning to what we experience. These APES are the epitome of black and white thinking; assumptions, perspectives, and expectations; that involve sweeping generalizations with only two existing options.

- Either I do a good job listening to my kids or I don't.
- Either my daughter is cooperative or she isn't.
- Either I can trust my judgment or I can't.
- Either I am a control freak or my kids are running amok.

With Either-Or APES, both options might feel like good ones: *Either I provide clear guidelines or I am supportive and nurturing……* Or one option might be desirable and the other undesirable: *Either I take care of myself or I fall apart…* And sometimes neither option feels right: *Either I keep being a demanding ogre or I turn into a pushover…*

Either-Or APES tend to come with **overwhelming implications** about the massive changes needed to CLEAN THINGS UP. This makes it easy to shut down with *I can't* before we even take the first step because that first step can be a real killer.

Examples

EITHER I clean the house from top to bottom OR I will be judged and found lacking

> **The OVERWHELMING IMPLICATION:** *Tonight will be awful. I need to pick Sam up from baseball in an hour. I have to get the chicken casserole started because the Smiths will be here at 6:00. I can't have guests over when my house looks like such a pig sty. I will have to run myself ragged to get it all done and then I'll be too tired to be a good host.*

EITHER I let my daughter go to the concert OR she'll hate me.

> **The OVERWHELMING IMPLICATION:** *I can't set limits. I can't trust my own judgment. I need to let my daughter call the shots or I'll ruin any chance I have to reestablish a speaking role in her life.*

EITHER I know what's best for my kids OR the world falls apart.

> **The OVERWHELMING IMPLICATION:** *So often I don't know what they need. What's the matter with me?! I am allowing my kids to be destroyed. I am unfit to be their mom. What am I going to do? I'm a horrible mother. I must have all the answers because look what's at stake.*

Aim Your Control, Control Your Aim.

EITHER I am a super parent OR I am a lousy parent.

The Overwhelming Implication: *If I am not a super parent then I must be a lousy parent. I have to leap the Grand Canyon to be the parent I want to be. Furthermore, until I have completed that (impossible) leap, I am wrong, I am bad, I am guilty of everything I have ever been accused of or accused myself of...*

The Either-Or perspective isn't wrong or 'bad'. There are undoubtedly times when it does the job quite nicely. If, however, this is our primary perspective, our primary filter for exploring, explaining, problem-solving, and assessing; life becomes a whole lot more difficult than it needs to be.

Exercise 3:4

1. Identify five of your Either-Or APES.
   - Either I... or...   Either she/he... or...   Either it... or
2. For each one, write the Overwhelming Implications.
3. Keep a running list and add to it each time you find yourself engaged in Either-Or thinking.
4. Choose "I will notice my Either-Or APES" as one of your **Paying Attention** practices.

The great thing about Either-Or is that it tends not to be a Law of Nature.

We make it up as we go along and therefore we can change it.

Section 3: In Charge of Me

A-ha 3:5

Continuums: Busting Open Either-Or

Characteristics, capabilities, wants, and needs all occur along vast continuums. And it is this perspective that helps us stop thinking in terms of Either-Or.

Consider the previously mentioned APE, *Either I am a super parent or I am a lousy parent*. I am either one or the other. And think about the overwhelming implication of what I need to do to arrive at the 'right' option, to become a super parent.

Viewed as a **continuum**, however, we have more options than **either** the euphoric feeling, *As a parent, I'm the greatest thing since sliced bread*, **or** the demoralizing feeling, *I am worthless as a parent*.

We can use continuums to figure out exactly where these high and low feelings are coming from and what we want to do about them.

> **FAQ:** Wait a minute. Why would I need to figure out where the positive feelings are coming from? What's wrong with feeling euphoric?
>
> Actually, there is nothing wrong with it. My computer crashes and, without really noticing what I'm doing, I jiggle a bunch of cables and wires, turn a bunch of doohickeys, and I get the computer to reboot. Now that's euphoria. And it sure beats the alternative. The drawback is that I am not sure what I did. I don't know my PROCESS so I have no additional knowledge to help me prevent the next crash or resolve it if it reoccurs.
>
> CONTINUUMS shift us further towards Intentional Self by increasing our awareness of our Parenting Process. And through this increased awareness we have more choice about what we will and won't do. The better we understand our Parenting Process the more power and control we have with respect to ourselves and the structure we provide our kids.

Continuums are sliding scales with infinite possibilities between two defined end points. They work like dimmer switches as opposed to on/off switches. We use continuums to expand our understanding by identifying Key Elements, factors that are important to us, that slide us along a continuum in either direction.

My Global Parenting Continuum with three Key Elements:

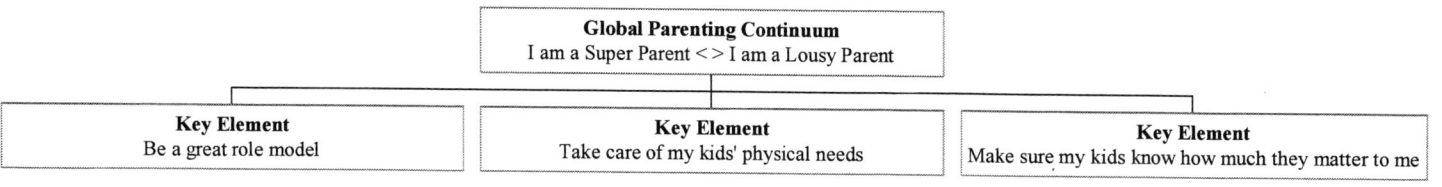

Global Parenting Continuum
I am a Super Parent < > I am a Lousy Parent

- **Key Element**: Be a great role model
- **Key Element**: Take care of my kids' physical needs
- **Key Element**: Make sure my kids know how much they matter to me

When seen on a continuum, I may be moving in one direction with one key element and in the opposite direction with another. Knowing this helps me choose what, if anything, I want to change. What I want to do more of or what I want to do less of. It shows me possibilities for doing things differently. And it shows me when to pat myself on the back!

Expanding Levels of the Continuum

I can expand this Continuum to another level and provide even more detail for exploration by defining each Key Element as a Sub-continuum with its own set of Key Elements.

We all know how it feels to have a generalized sense of dread or anxiety, those times when we can't figure out what's causing it but we feel just awful. The more we are able to pin-point the source of the uncomfortable feelings the less overwhelming they are. The easier it is to see what we can do about them.

Identifying Continuums, Key Elements, and Sub-continuums helps us pin-point....

My Global Parenting Continuum expanded to another level

Parent Continuum
I am a Super Parent < > I am a Lousy Parent

Key Element A
Be a great role model

Key Element B
Take care of my kids' physical needs

Key Element C
Make sure my kids know how much they matter to me

Sub-Continuum 1
I am a great role model < >Heaven forbid my kids turn out like me

Sub-Continuum 2
I provide for my kids' physical needs < > I don't do enough

Sub-Continuum 3
I let my kids know how important they are to me< >I ignore my kids

Key Element Compassionate
a.

Key Element Patient
b.

Key Element Organized
c.

Key Element Cook Dinner
d.

Key Element Clean
e.

Key Element Make doctor appointments
f.

Key Element Listen to them
g.

Key Element Attend games
h.

Key Element Consider kids' opinions
i.

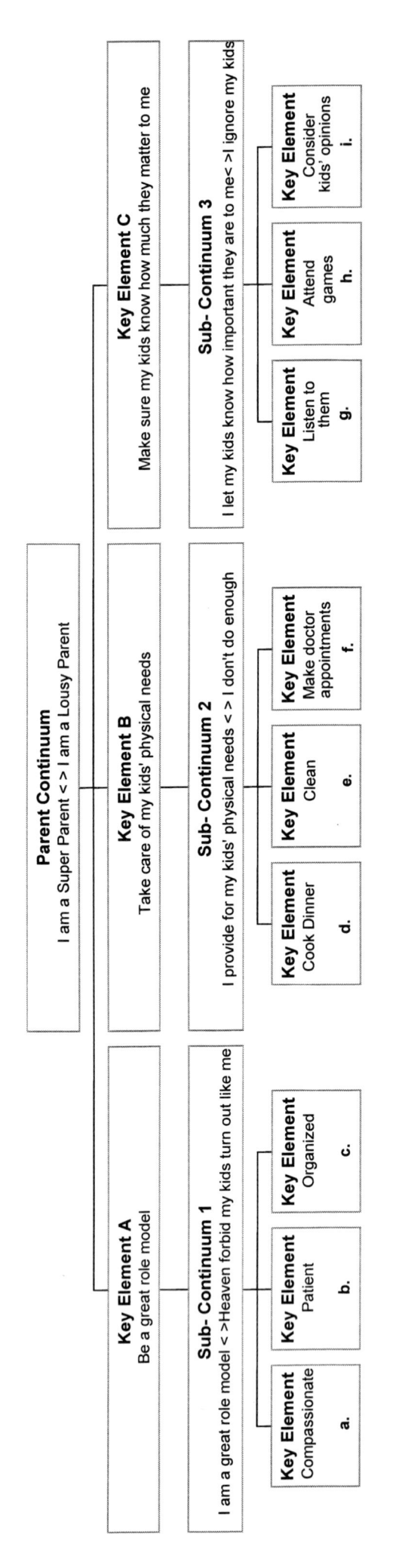

We can expand indefinitely…

Aim Your Control, Control Your Aim.

> **FAQ: Why would I keep expanding the levels?**
>
> Think of that computer and setting up your file system in Windows Explorer. The more folders and sub-folders you create, the easier it is to find what you are looking for. Or if you are a non-computer type, it is the difference between having a stack of papers piled a mile high on your desk and having a well organized file cabinet.
>
> The more we expand, the easier it is to find what we're looking for...

When we use continuums and key elements to explore, explain, problem-solve, and assess, we realize we are doing splendidly in some areas, good enough in some, and perhaps miserably in others.

Important note about Continuums:

As with Either-Or APES, we may perceive one end of the continuum as desirable and the other end as undesirable:

> I am emotionally available < > I am emotionally unavailable

We may also have continuums with two perceived undesirable ends:

> I am a dictator < > I am wishy-washy

And our continuums may have two desirable ends that compete for our resources; our attention, time, and money.

> I take care of my kids < > I make time for me

By the way, look at the **OVERWHELMING IMPLICATIONS** if these were Either-Or APES. The first one would be exhausting as we tried to achieve or maintain the 'desirable' option all the time. The second one would put us between a rock and a hard place. And the third one would be a horrible choice to have to make.

Changing Either-Or APES into Continuums and Key Elements gives us more options for being the parents we want to be.

Section 3: In Charge of Me

Exercise 3:5

Using **Exercise 3:5 Example** on page 59 as a guide, complete the **Practice Sheet** on page 60 following these six steps:

1. Write a brief description of one thing you feel you aren't doing well enough in your role as parent.
2. Turn it into an Either-Or statement.
3. Identify it as a continuum.
   (label the ends of the continuum with the 'Either' and the 'Or')
4. Write down three Key Elements that are part of this continuum.
5. Expand each of these Key Elements into sub-continuums.
6. Write down three Key Elements for each sub-continuum.

Repeat Steps 1-6 with three other roles you play... spouse, partner, sibling, child, professional...

Do Steps 1-6 again for each role you chose with respect to things you are doing great with, things you are proud of.

This is not an easy exercise. Don't worry about getting all the words right. Trust what pops up and write it down, recognizing when it gets hardest in order to learn more about your process for busting open Either-Or APES.

Learning to shift perspective and to stop thinking in Either-Or requires deliberate practice. The more we practice, the easier it gets. And the more continuums become our standard way of looking at the world, the more effectively we can explore, explain, problem- solve, and make assessments.

Because they expand the degree of possibility, continuums help us be more flexible and adaptable.

Exercise 3:5 Example
Busting open Either-Or with Continuums

Step 1 Brief description of what I want to explore:

I wonder if I provide enough guidance for my kids.... I get confused sometimes about trusting what I know as the mom and being open to their alternative viewpoints and perspectives...

Step 2 Stated as an Either-Or:

Either I am a dictator Or I am wishy-washy

Step 3 Identified as a Continuum:

I'm a dictator < > I'm wishy-washy

Step 4 Key Elements of this Continuum:

Key Element (**A**): Keep my kids safe

Key Element (**B**): Allow my kids to learn from their mistakes

Key Element (**C**): Respect my kids' opinions

Steps 5 & 6 Key Elements expanded into Sub-Continuums and Key Elements

Key Element (A) as a Sub-Continuum
Keep my kids safe < > Be over protective

   Key Elements of this Sub-Continuum:
   (1) Know where they are
   (2) Discuss critical issues with them
   (3) Establish effective rules

Key Element (B) as a Sub-Continuum
Allow my kids to learn from their mistakes < > Let them take too many risks

   Key Elements of this Sub-Continuum:
   (1) Trust their judgments
   (2) Check for understanding
   (3) Know when to intervene

Key Element (C) as a Sub-Continuum
I respect my kids' opinions < > I refuse to listen

   Key Elements of this Sub-Continuum:
   (1) Stay flexible
   (2) Be willing to question and challenge
   (3) Be prepared to draw the line

Section 3: In Charge of Me

Exercise 3:5 Practice Sheet

Step 1 Brief description of what I want to explore:

Step 2 Stated as an Either/Or:

    Either: Or:

Step 3: Identified as a Continuum:

_____ < > _____

Step 4: Key Elements of this Continuum:

    Key Element (A):
    Key Element (B):
    Key Element (C):

Steps 5 & 6: Key Elements expanded into Sub-Continuums and Key Elements

                Key Element (A) as a Sub-Continuum

_____ < > _____

Key Elements of Sub-Continuum (A):
a.
b.
c.

                Key Element (B) as a Sub-Continuum

_____ < > _____

Key Elements of Sub-Continuum (B).
a.
b.
c.

                Key Element (C) as a Sub-Continuum

_____ < > _____

Key Elements of Sub-Continuum (C)
a.
b.
c.

Aim Your Control, Control Your Aim.

| A-ha 3:6 |

Shifts:
Moving Along Our Continuums

Irma: How long did it take you to eat so healthy?
Sally: I have no idea. It just sort of happened over time and here I am.

Being the parents we want to be is a lot like that. It's often a slow process versus big, life altering changes we can identify. Our movements along the Control Continuum, our movements back and forth between Automatic Pilot and Intentional Self, primarily happen through gradual changes we make or small changes we need to make and don't.

Change can be frightening and difficult. Change is most overwhelming when we have not volunteered for it or when the change is bigger than we are prepared for.

That's where **shifts** come in. **Shifts** are the changes we choose to make that move us along our continuums.

The Advantage of Shifts

Shifts maximize our sense of control because we define the continuums along which we are shifting and we decide on the size and timing of the shifts.

With shifts, we don't have to turn the proverbial sow's ear into a silk purse unless we are ready to do so. And we certainly don't need to do it in one fell swoop.

Shifts can be small steps... *Last year I went to four softball games, this season I'll go to seven...* And they can be Grand Canyon-style leaps... *I won't miss any of this summer's twenty-six games.*

> **The change process is a lot less intimidating when we realize we have this much control over it.**

Section 3: In Charge of Me

What is Shift-able?

We can shift our **APES**, our **Actions**, and our **Measurement Strategies** as long as we turn off the Automatic Pilot and know what our APES, Actions, and Measurement Strategies are.

Example

My Global Parenting Continuum

I am a Super Parent < > I am a Lousy Parent

Sub Continuum #3

I let my kids know how important they are < > I ignore my kids

Key Element (g.)

Listen to them

My APES and Actions with respect to this Key Element

I was really distracted today when Katie called. I was sitting in front of the computer and not really attending to what she was telling me. In general, I think I get overwhelmed with all the stuff I have to get done. I don't always make the time or always remember to give her my undivided attention when she's talking to me. Having others listen to me is really important to me. It's part of my trusting and being willing to open up. Listening to my daughters is a big part of how I show them they matter, both as my kids and as people...

My Measurement Strategy

How often Sarah and Katie ask for my perspective and my opinion, and how much they share with me.

Possible Shifts I Could Make

Shifts I might choose that would move me towards "I let my kids know how important they are" which moves me towards "Super Parent":

- I could turn away from the computer when I am working and one of the kids calls me.
- I could ask them each day what's going on and remind myself to pay attention to what they say.
- I could set aside one hour of uninterrupted kid-conversation each week.
- Or I could realize that listening to my kids is one of the ways I really do show they are important and that listening to my kids is one of the ways I really am doing a super job as mom.

   It could be that having noticed how I am doing with respect to this Key Element was enough of a reminder for me and there is nothing else I choose to do about it right now, nothing else I choose to shift.

Sometimes just Paying Attention to our APES, Actions, and Measurement Strategies is the very shift needed to move us in the direction we want to go.

An Example with Even Greater Detail

Shifts I have made with respect to body image. Viewing it as a continuum it becomes:
Taking care of my body < > Being unrealistic and completely neurotic

APES Shifts

Oh yeah, now I get it (The Spin I put on it)

From: I can absolutely control how my body will look

To: Of course a healthy body will not look the same at different ages

What I believe to be true (Assumptions)

From: If I exercise and eat really healthy, my body should be perfect

To: I am never again going to have the body of a 21-year-old

How I encourage or defeat myself (Perspectives)

From: I have blown everything by eating that piece of cheesecake

To: I have not done ever-lasting damage to my body, my health, or my fitness by eating that box of Thin Mints

What I resolve for the future (Expectations)

From: I will be toned, cut, and solid when I am ninety

To: I will be healthy and fit when I am ninety

Action Shift:
What I do

From: I only choose food with extremely minimal fat content

To: I eat a larger variety of foods while being aware of overall fat intake

Measurement Strategy Shift:
What I attend to that informs me of my progress

From: How I look

To: How I feel

Note: Look what would happen had I left this as an Either-Or APE.

Either my 52-year-old body would look like it did when I was twenty-one **Or** it would need fixing. The **overwhelming implication** is I would have spent the next forty years miserably striving for an unattainable goal.

Section 3: In Charge of Me

Exercise 3:6

Using Exercise 3:6 Practice Sheet:

1. Choose one of your continuums from **Exercise 3:5**
2. For one of its Key Elements write down your APES, Actions, and Measurement Strategies. Write whatever comes to mind.
3. Describe one mini-shift, one mid-size shift, and one Grand Canyon-style shift with respect to each type of shift (APES, Actions, and Measurement Strategies).

Don't get bogged down worrying about the 'right' words or only writing down shifts you would actually be willing to make. The purpose of this exercise is to gain a better understanding about the scope of shifts we can choose to make with respect to size and type. So let go of any restrictions you might put on yourself and get really outrageous.

Exercise 3:6 Practice Sheet

The Continuum I am Standing On:

_____ < > _____

The Key Element:

My Current APES, Actions, and Measurement Strategies with respect to this Key Element:
(What you believe with respect to this Key Element, what actions you are currently taking, and what you focus on to assess how you are doing.)

Possible Shifts:

APES

A Mini-Shift:

A Mid-Size Shift:

A Grand Canyon-Style Shift:

Actions

A Mini-Shift:

A Mid-Size Shift:

A Grand Canyon-Style Shift:

Measurement Strategies

A Mini-Shift:

A Mid-Size Shift:

A Grand Canyon-Style Shift:

Section 3: In Charge of Me

A-ha 3:7

Worrying is a Choice

A Story

I am a worrier... This has shown up loudest in my mom-hood... Way up there on the worry scale are car accidents... I was the mom who lay awake until I knew both kids were home safely... for years... and years. Until the morning I woke up having fallen asleep without knowing... And was instantly overcome with GUILT. I didn't get what, but I 'knew' I had done something terribly wrong.

After a lot of gentle soul searching, I realized that for me worrying meant caring... I had this huge APE that said if I didn't worry then I didn't love my daughters... And shining the light on THAT foolishness allowed me to let it go because that just wasn't true.

From there came the really cool A-ha that worrying was indeed a choice. That I could actually choose not to worry. And I have gotten better with it over time.

As parents, the thought of not worrying can seem as far-fetched as having a magic lamp with our own personal genie. But we can get better at it through awareness and practice. And the better we get at it, the more able we are to stay in the Reality with the Automatic Pilot switch turned off. (Not to mention what a relief it is to not worry so much.)

Exercise 3:7

1. Start a Worry Log

2. For one week, write down everything you worry about. Pay attention to your APES and your emotions. Include any physical reactions that help you know you are worrying.

3. Keep the log by your bed in case you wake up in the middle of the night in a cold sweat about something.

4. Look for patterns and evidence of your Catch 22s.

5. Name five things you used to worry about but no longer do.

6. Can you identify what helped you stop?

7. Write for ten minutes about the connection between worrying and control.

And don't worry about not being able to stop worrying. That's much too counter-productive!

Aim Your Control, Control Your Aim.

A-ha 3:8

Those Pesky WhatIfs

Much of our worry about the quality of our parenting can be translated into the WhatIfs. And these WhatIfs can very quickly shift us to Automatic Pilot and into the Illusion of Control.

- WhatIf I don't let her go and she never speaks to me again?
- WhatIf I should have been more adamant?
- WhatIf I'm being too strict?
- WhatIf I make a mistake?
- WhatIf I'm not really strict enough?
- WhatIf I'm not considering her perspective on it?
- WhatIf I can't help her understand?

Having a process for facing the WhatIfs head-on will keep them from having unforeseen power and control over you.

Exercise 3:8

Step 1 Take a specific entry from your Worry Log (**Exercise 3:7**) and turn it into a WhatIf statement.

Step 2 Really ask yourself the following questions, being open to any answers that show up. Write it out, talk it out, think it out… Whatever works best for you.

Q1 What if this WhatIf comes to pass?

Allow yourself to see and FEEL the absolute worst possibility. Sink into it and don't stop seeing it and feeling it until it is done being seen and felt. Trust that you'll know when it's done. You'll feel a release.

Q2 What do I really know about this WhatIf?

Where does it come from? When else has it worried me? What else does it represent or is it standing in for? How does it help me?

Q3 What have I already done to prevent it or minimize the likelihood of it occurring?

Be honest and generous with all the details…

Section 3: In Charge of Me

Q4 Is there anything else I can do to prevent it or minimize its likelihood?

> Go for broke... identify all the possibilities that seem both within your power and outside of it...

Step 3 If the answer to **Q4** is yes, choose which of the listed actions you will do and then do them.

If you get stuck trying to do what you've chosen, repeat Steps 2 and 3 with the WhatIfs that are getting in your way...

Step 4 If the answer to **Q4** is no, make friends with your worry by honestly answering the following question:

Q5 What does worrying about this WhatIf teach me?

> The more we hate our worrying the more we cut ourselves off from a part of ourselves. The more we fight against the worrying, the more we block the answers and the lessons it has for us.
>
> Worrying can be a huge help in shifting us towards Intentional Self. When we are not battling it, we can use it as a reminder to pay attention and to be really present to what we have no control over. We can use it to help us face our fears and move beyond them. Worrying can be just the signal we need to take action including the action of letting go. And it may be a signal to remember what we know with certainty.

For more practice, choose three other entries from your Worry Log and repeat Steps 1 through 4.

The more you practice this process the more you'll discover exactly what helps you face and let go of your WhatIf worries. Through practice, you will discover your own steps and questions.

Just remember, everyone can move beyond the WhatIfs. We each just need to find the way that works best for us.

And there will always be WhatIfs. There will always be a zillion more things we don't know and can't predict than things we can know for sure.

The trick is to have a process for turning each WhatIf into a WhatIs...

When you notice yourself worrying about the WhatIfs, pull yourself back to the present by reminding yourself about a single WhatIs for which you are grateful.

Aim Your Control, Control Your Aim.

| A-ha 3:9 |

Curb Your Impatience

A Story

As this book got closer and closer to completion, I found myself getting really impatient. After working on it contentedly forever, **I WANTED IT TO BE DONE YESTERDAY**. I wanted it completed so I could move on to the next book. And as ready as I was to have it be finished, I noticed myself doing so much that was preventing me from finishing it…

You might find yourself getting impatient as you discover new things about yourself. As you understand more about your kids and begin utilizing new parenting strategies. You might start out highly motivated and excited and then start wondering why you are not 'there' yet.

Maintaining our self-awareness throughout this process and shifting our APES with respect to impatience, enables us to keep moving forward and achieve our goals. Three things to keep in mind about impatience:

A. Impatience is actually a powerful indicator that you are getting closer to where you are going.

Recognizing this helps us see our impatience as a positive sign.

Think about how true this is. Spending years discovering what you are meant to be doing and when you finally have it figured out **YOU WANT TO BE DOING IT**… Looking for that special someone and then she/he shows up… The last class in your Master's program… Having your planned vacation six months away, then a week away… The ninth month of your pregnancy… The last five minutes of so many things… We get impatient as we get closer.

B. The closer we get to our goal the more our fear kicks in.

Recognizing the fear prevents it from stopping us.

This takes us right back to the WhatIfs:

- WhatIf it doesn't happen this time?
- WhatIf I can't go the distance?
- WhatIf I never really get there?
- WhatIf I'm not doing all I am supposed to be doing?
- WhatIf this has all been a big misunderstanding or a huge mistake?
- WhatIf I missed something important along the way?
- WhatIf I get there and it's not what I expected?

Section 3: In Charge of Me

C. The closer we get to where we are going the more things speed up, the faster our doubts fly at us and the more we race to get there.

Recognizing this speed-up prevents the Runaway Train Syndrome.

This allows us to slow down and create room for the next step and to remember how far we've come. Slowing down prevents us from cutting crucial corners as we race to the finish line. When we don't recognize the speed-up we forfeit a great deal of control over our own growth and development.

Exercise 3:9

1. Notice your impatience with respect to A-ha Parenting.
    a. What do you wish you were able to do **RIGHT NOW**?
    b. What do you wish was happening **RIGHT NOW**?

2. For each thing you are impatient about, identify how much closer you are now than you were before you started this journey with Irma.

3. Describe what has enhanced your progress so far and what has impeded it. This will give you more choice as you move forward.

4. Explain how 'there' will be different from 'here'. This vision will help you keep going when the going gets tough.

5. Identify which WhatIfs are scaring you. This will allow you to check out the veracity of the WhatIfs and use **Exercise 3:8** to transform each of your WhatIfs into the corresponding WhatIs.

Note: Transforming each WhatIf into the WhatIs enables us to stay focused on the present which is where all the growth and development take place.

Note: Frustration and Impatience

Pay special attention to the subtle difference between frustration and impatience. Frustration involves something missing or something not going right. With impatience, the only thing missing or not going right is how darned long it's all taking.

If you feel frustrated with respect to your understanding and implementation of what you are learning, reflect on these questions:

1. What could you be doing more of (or less of) to get to where you want to be?
2. What's holding you back? Is it an assumption? An expectation? A story you're telling yourself?
3. What are you forgetting?
4. What additional support do you need?
5. How can you get it?

> **FAQ: But what if I can't tell the difference between frustration and impatience?**
>
> Don't worry about it! If what you read about impatience helped, then assume you're impatient. If what you read about frustration got you thinking, then there's probably some frustration and you should reflect upon the above questions.
>
> What we call it is not as important as noticing what keeps us moving forward into being the kind of parents we want to be.

Section 3: In Charge of Me

A-ha 3:10

Clarify Your Intention

Check out this conversation:

Chad: I want to stop being so stubborn.

Irma: What do you mean by stubborn?

Chad: I'm not sure.

Irma: Okay, what are you doing when you are being stubborn?

Chad: I have to show my kids I'm right, I have to prove that I am right.

Irma: So when you're being stubborn, what aren't you doing?

Chad: I am not listening or considering their point of view.

Irma: Got it. So what would it look like, what will you be doing when you are being less stubborn?

Chad: I'll be listening better; truly considering and trying to understand what my kids are trying to tell me.

Irma: Yeah, I bet that would really help. How will you know you're doing that?

Chad: I'll be asking questions to help me understand what they are trying to tell me. I won't be responding so quickly after they say something. I'll be quiet more as I think about what they just said.

Irma: Great. How else will you know when you are being less stubborn?

Chad: I might change my mind more often as they tell me new things. I won't feel so angry like I do when I'm determined to prove they are wrong. I'll be focusing more on trying to understand what they are saying that might be right. Cool.

Irma: Very Cool

Exercise 3:10

1. Name one thing you'd like to change about you or your parenting right now. Something you want to stop or start doing; something you want to do more or less of.

2. Using the above dialogue as a guide, play both parts. Ask yourself the questions that will help you clarify your intentions, what it is you really want to accomplish, and how you will know when you have accomplished it.

Aim Your Control, Control Your Aim.

A-ha 3:11

Be the Changes

Parenting is the most sacred thing we do. And it can certainly be the most challenging. As parents, our days are filled with decisions and crammed with paradox:

Protect our kids at all costs • Let them learn the hard way
Keep them close • Set them free
Take care of them • Make time for me
Love them to death • Keep me from killing them!

What worked yesterday or last year, doesn't work any more. What felt like support to one kid has the opposite impact on another or on the same kid ten minutes later.

So how do we stay calm in the midst of all this turmoil? How do we stay afloat despite the swift currents of change threatening to pull us under? How do we gain clarity within all the confusion? How do we stay open to our kids' unique energy and aliveness?

➢ We spend a lifetime loving, learning, and laughing at how bizarre it all can be.

➢ We keep shifting towards Intentional Self to discover what works.

➢ We stay focused on the Reality and making the shifts that allow us to parent from there.

And we remember that what we DO has a lot more impact on our kids than what we SAY…

- The more our actions demonstrate awareness of self and others, the more aware our kids become.

- The more our actions demonstrate that perfection is not necessary and we learn from our mistakes, the more our kids come to accept this too.

- The more our actions demonstrate responsibility and an understanding of what can and should be controlled, the more our kids come to internalize responsibility.

- The more our actions demonstrate a total belief in our kids, the more they come to believe in themselves.

Section 3: In Charge of Me

Whatever it is we want our kids to learn, turning off our Automatic Pilot and standing in the Reality enables us to know it, live it, and successfully teach it… As Gandhi said, "We must be the changes we wish to see in the world."

Exercise 3:11

1. Write down what you really want your kids to learn, what you really want your kids to become.

2. Keep a running Do-as-I-Do Parenting Log. List all the ways you are **modeling** what you want your kids to learn and become.

3. Keep a running Do-as-I-Say Parenting Log. List all the ways your actions don't match your intentions and words.

4. What shifts do you want to make in order to expand the Do-as-I-Do log and shrink the Do-as-I-Say log?

Aim Your Control, Control Your Aim.

IN CHARGE OF ME
Check In

Exercise 3:1 **What Makes Shifting So Hard?**

☐ **Ah, I did it**

It helped   It didn't help   I don't know, I need to keep going

☐ **Oh, I didn't do it**

It was too hard   I didn't have time   Other_____

Exercise 3:2 **My Catch 22**

☐ **Ah, I did it**

It helped   It didn't help   I don't know, I need to keep going

☐ **Oh, I didn't do it**

It was too hard   I didn't have time   Other_____

Exercise 3:3 **Paying Attention**

☐ **Ah, I did it**

It helped   It didn't help   I don't know, I need to keep going

☐ **Oh, I didn't do it**

It was too hard   I didn't have time   Other_____

Section 3: In Charge of Me

Exercise 3:4 **Either-Or**

☐ **Ah, I did it**

It helped   It didn't help   I don't know, I need to keep going

☐ **Oh, I didn't do it**

It was too hard   I didn't have time   Other_____

Exercise 3:5 **Continuums: Busting Open Either-Or**

☐ **Ah, I did it**

It helped   It didn't help   I don't know, I need to keep going

☐ **Oh, I didn't do it**

It was too hard   I didn't have time   Other_____

Exercise 3:6 **Shifts: Moving Along My Continuums**

☐ **Ah, I did it**

It helped   It didn't help   I don't know, I need to keep going

☐ **Oh, I didn't do it**

It was too hard   I didn't have time   Other_____

Exercise 3:7 **Worrying is a Choice**

☐ **Ah, I did it**

It helped   It didn't help   I don't know, I need to keep going

☐ **Oh, I didn't do it**

It was too hard   I didn't have time   Other_____

Exercise 3:8 **Those Pesky WhatIfs**

☐ **Ah, I did it**

It helped   It didn't help   I don't know, I need to keep going

☐ **Oh, I didn't do it**

It was too hard   I didn't have time   Other_____

Exercise 3:9 **Curb Your Impatience**

☐ **Ah, I did it**

It helped   It didn't help   I don't know, I need to keep going

☐ **Oh, I didn't do it**

It was too hard   I didn't have time   Other_____

Exercise 3:10 **Clarify Your Intention**

☐ **Ah, I did it**

It helped   It didn't help   I don't know, I need to keep going

☐ **Oh, I didn't do it**

It was too hard   I didn't have time   Other_____

Exercise 3:11 **Be the Changes**

☐ **Ah, I did it**

It helped   It didn't help   I don't know, I need to keep going

☐ **Oh, I didn't do it**

It was too hard   I didn't have time   Other_____

What else helps you remember that You are In Charge of You?

Notes

When our anger, frustration, and fear
blindside us and take over the control panel
we are far less likely to be heard.

Because HOW we say it is as important as WHAT it is we say.

Section 4

Create the Reality

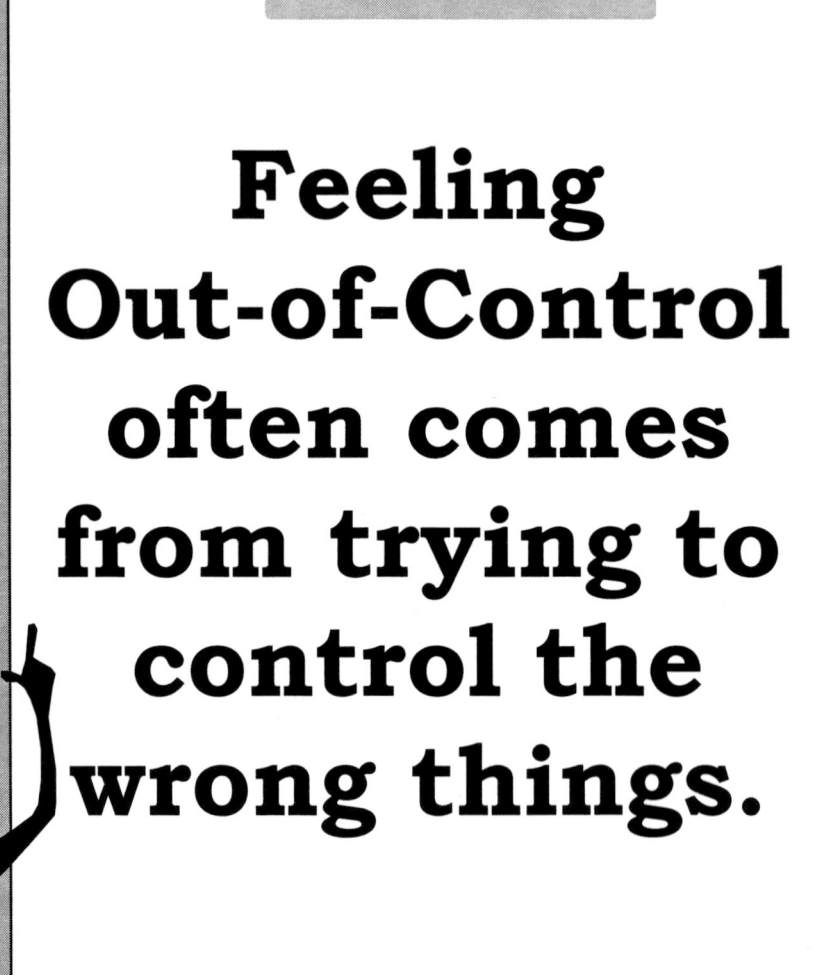

Feeling Out-of-Control often comes from trying to control the wrong things.

Section 4: Create the Reality

Prevention and Intervention

The strategies in this section are things you can do, actions you can take, to create the Reality in your home. Many of these strategies will be familiar to you; many of them are already part of your Parenting Process.

Shifting further towards Intentional Self and raising these strategies to a conscious level of awareness gives you the power to choose when and how to use them. Like the previous computer example, knowing which doohickey we twisted to reboot the computer enables us to try it again the next time the computer crashes.

In addition, the more aware we are of what improves communication and increases cooperation and ownership, the more skillfully we can teach our kids strategies to navigate their worlds efficiently and effectively.

Each strategy in this section serves as both Prevention and Intervention…

The Strategies as Prevention

When these strategies are part of our ongoing Parenting Process they help us stand in the Reality on a minute-to-minute, day-to-day basis. Implemented this way, they maximize our kids' growth and success, build mutual trust, and open up the channels for effective communication.

When fully integrated into our parenting, these strategies empower our kids in positive ways so there is less need for them to act out with unhealthy choices and behaviors. It becomes less likely that our kids will spin too far out-of-control.

The Strategies as Interventions

These strategies are also actions we can take when things get tough, when our kids are having a particularly rough time.

Used as an Intervention, they show our kids that we are able to help them, take care of them, and be there for them, without cutting them off at the knees. As Intervention Strategies, they minimize the 'us-against-them' feelings and end perceived battles more quickly.

Section 4: Create the Reality

Another way to explain it...

You can eat salad because it is part of your stay-healthy diet and you can eat salad to lose weight for your 15th High School Reunion which is two weeks away.

Prevention... Intervention... Same Action!

The more we incorporate these strategies into our parenting the less they will be needed as interventions and the more adept we are at using them when things do get difficult. As a matter of fact, the more we incorporate them into our everyday parenting the less we find ourselves defining things as 'difficult'. Having successful strategies that we are comfortable using truly does make parenting easier.

The Following 25 Strategies will:

> **Maximize your sense of control**
>
> **Maximize your kids' sense of control**
>
> **Help you make the *Reality* a reality**

Possibilities for moving through this section:

1. The Strategies as Prevention:

a. Take the strategies in order, practicing and reflecting on one or two per week.

OR

b. Try each one for a day or two, returning to those you want more practice with after you have worked through all of them.

2. The Strategies as Intervention:

- Make a list of specific challenges you are facing.
- Choose one of these issues.
- Read through all the strategies
- Select the one(s) that might help you address the chosen issue.
- Practice with the selected strategy (strategies) until you are comfortable with them and/or until you have resolved the issue.
- Move on to other challenges and other strategies.

A Control Continuum Reminder:

In order to use these strategies you need to **shift** your **focus** from trying to control (change) your kids to controlling (choosing) what you will say and do.

STRATEGY 1
Shift to a Learning Stance

We shift to a Learning Stance by moving out of the role of 'The Adult with All the Answers'. We stop Teaching and Advising and start asking **Expansion Questions**: Questions we really wonder about as we observe and interact with our kids. Questions that clarify. Questions that invite our kids to discover and share their own APES.

A Story

Sarah called to ask for my advice as she prepared an activity for her 3rd graders

> **Sarah**: Mom, help me think of a story I can use from my childhood.
> **Me**: Tell them about the time you played Bozo Buckets.
> **Sarah**: No, not that one.
> **Me**: Tell them about when you got lost at Oak Brook Mall.
> **Sarah**: Nah, that won't work.
> **Me**: Tell them about…
> **Sarah**: Hmmm, I don't think that's the best one.

She'd asked for advice, I gave it my best shot, and none of the suggestions hit the mark. I stopped trying to give answers, took a step back, and got real curious about what she was looking for:

- What are you trying to model for the kids?
- What do you want them to understand?
- What do you want to give them permission to do?
- What do you want them to know about you?
- What do you want them to discover about themselves?

After a five minute discussion, Sarah came up with the best story to share with her kids.

> **Shifting to a Learning Stance
> helps our kids come up with their own answers and solutions…**

Example

Your son comes to you in a state of rage about what a teacher did to him that morning. You start trying to advise or teach…

> "She's only trying to help you."
> "She needs more information. Try telling her your side."
> "You shouldn't feel that way because you instigated it."

Section 4: Create the Reality

But your child is too agitated to hear you… too upset to let anything you're saying penetrate…

You have options:

1. Keep trying to do what you're doing
i.e. banging your head against the same brick wall!
(Refer to **Section 6 Power Struggles**)

2. Throw your hands up in frustration and say,
"So what do you want from me?"

3. Or stop trying to give answers and get truly inquisitive about his perspective.
"What's the worst part?"
"What have you already tried doing about this?"
"What are you hoping will happen?"
"What do you want your teacher to do?"
"What do you want her to understand?"

> **Shifting to a Learning Stance
> gives us a better understanding of which of our answers and suggestions
> might be the most helpful.**

When to consider shifting to a Learning Stance

1. When you sense there's something else going on besides what your child is saying.

2. When you are not sure what the real question is.

3. When you are frustrated or confused.

4. When you find your child blaming others and making excuses.

5. When you are not sure if there is a real problem that needs addressing or if you are simply observing something that is different than what you want or expect.

6. When you've lost sight of the Big Picture.

7. When there is a lot of 'yes, but-ting' and 'I've already tried that' going on.

8. When it feels like you are working really hard just to *MAKE* your child hear you.

One way to shift to a Learning Stance is to notice what question your next response would answer and ASK THE QUESTION INSTEAD!

Example: Instead of saying, "You should have walked away" you would ask, "What else could you have done?"

> **By the way, as with many of the Create the Reality Strategies,
> Shifting to a Learning Stance works with
> spouses, co-workers, bosses, the insurance agent, our mothers…**

Strategy 1
Shift to a Learning Stance

Tips & Check In

- ✓ Ask yourself if having more information would help you know what needs to come next.
- ✓ Decide if the best 'answer' is actually a question.
- ✓ Let go of the need to be IN CHARGE.
- ✓ Stay curious, stop trying to prove a point or teach something.
- ✓ Listen to your child's answers with a receptive mind and an open heart.
- ✓ Identify what APES and fears pop up as you Shift to a Learning Stance.
- ✓ Notice how much more your kids show you, share with you, when you Shift to a Learning Stance.

When have you Shifted to a Learning Stance?

How did it work?

Describe a situation where this strategy would have come in handy.

How will this strategy surprise your kids?

When might it annoy them?

Notes:

Section 4: Create the Reality

STRATEGY 2

Let them have it
(the responsibility that is)

Examples

Uh-Oh Parenting

Sally remarks to a friend: Jason's teacher gives US way too much homework.

And this APE sure shows up in the miserable time after school while Sally tries to MAKE SURE that 10-year-old Jason does his homework. As soon as he walks in Sally takes his assignment sheet out of his book bag, spends the next two hours screaming and cajoling to get him to do his homework, and scrutinizes every paper for accuracy and completion.

Sally is certainly working hard to make sure THEY get good grades!

> **We do a disservice to our kids when we don't let them be responsible for what is rightfully their responsibility.**

A-Ha Parenting

Sally: This after school business is really horrible for both of us. What can we do to make it better?

Jason: I don't know. I hate when you're always yelling at me about homework.

Sally: Yeah, I hate it too. When is the best time for you to do your homework?

Jason: After dinner. Then I could do other things when I get home.

Sally: That seems too late with all the other things going on after dinner. I'd like you to get it done before you watch TV or go outside with your buddies. But I also get that after a whole day in school you might need a break before starting. How long of a break do you think would work?

Jason: A half hour

Sally: Okay. So at 4:00 you sit down and do your homework, right?

Jason: Yeah

Sally: Do you want me to remind you of the time or will you keep track of it?

Jason: I want you to remind me. ONCE!

Sally: What do you want me to do after that?

Jason: Leave me alone. I'll do it.

Sally: Okay. Would it be helpful for me to eyeball your homework after you finish it?

Jason: Sure

Sally: So we have an after school plan that'll help you at school and make stuff around here much nicer. I do need one thing from you. I'd like to schedule a time to sit down again and see how this is going. How about one week from today?

> **When A-ha Parenting Conversations are the
> very foundation of your relationship,
> so many other things just fall into place!**

Catch 22's and Letting Them Have It

By their very nature, Catch 22s can cause us to assume all sorts of responsibility that rightfully belongs to our kids. It is important to recognize when this happens so we can shift the responsibility back to our kids.

Shifting to a Learning Stance and Letting Them Have It

"Here's what I think you should do to fix it. Here's what we will do."

"I get this is tough for you. What can I do to help?"

By giving our kids answers and advice we take responsibility for finding solutions, and ultimately perhaps, for the problems themselves. By Shifting to a Learning Stance we can hand them the responsibility for figuring it out and, in the process, increase their sense of responsibility for how they got there in the first place.

It's important to keep responsibility in mind when we decide whether we will Teach, Advise, or Shift to a Learning Stance.

Section 4: Create the Reality

Strategy 2
Let them have it

Tips & Check In

✓ List all the responsibilities you would you like to shift from your shoulders to theirs.

✓ Identify what stops you for each one.

✓ Write down the benefits to you and your child for each responsibility you shift.

✓ Don't let fear, busy-ness, or confusion keep you from Letting them have it.

When is it easiest to give your kids responsibility?

When is it hardest?

What messages do your words and actions send about responsibility?

What does your child wish he/she could do?

List the responsibilities that go along with this.

Have an **A-ha Parenting Conversation** with your child around these responsibilities.

Notes:

Aim Your Control, Control Your Aim.

STRATEGY 3

Put it on the table

A Story

Sometimes I ask Katie to "call me when she gets there". Sometimes I don't. Sometimes she's more than willing to call. Sometimes it annoys her. Like the night she exclaimed, "I don't get it. Why do I have to call some times and not others?" I admitted my inconsistency and explained that, "To the best of my understanding, it seemed to have to do with when I felt vulnerable or afraid". Afterwards, Katie was much more open and much less irritated by these intermittent requests.

We get frustrated with our kids for not getting it and for not looking beyond their own feelings and needs. Yet how often are we expecting them to be mind readers?

> **Acknowledging what we are feeling
> gives our kids the opportunity to understand.**

More Examples

Your 5-year-old is stomping around the house. He won't tell you what he's looking for. No, he **"DOES NOT WANT YOUR HELP SEARCHING."** He isn't getting anywhere as he keeps looking in the same places over and over...

"Boy do I get how frustrating it is when you can't find what you're lookin' for..."

Your daughter walks in after school, sits at the kitchen table, and won't say a word. She slams the spoon down. She snaps when you ask if she'd like more granola. Her eyes start to fill up with tears...

"I get that you don't feel like talking right now, but if you change your mind I'm here..."

The dishwasher broke, your arm is sore, the kids are fighting; overall, it has been a really lousy morning...

"Hey kids, I'm feeling pretty frazzled right now, real close to the edge... Do you suppose a little break might be possible?"

> **When there is an obvious, unnamed elephant in the room
> and you put it on the table you can feel the energy shift.**

89

Section 4: Create the Reality

Strategy 3
Put it on the table

Tips & Check In

✓ Putting it on the table requires awareness and trust.

✓ Figure out what keeps you from sharing your feelings and/or observations.

✓ Decide if the reasons are acceptable to you.

✓ If they aren't, identify 3 steps you can take that will help you share more.

✓ Recognize the support you need in order to share more and ask for it.

✓ Remember that appropriately Putting it on the table is great role modeling.

Give an example of when you have successfully Put it on the table.

―――――

Give an example of when you have Put it on the table and it backfired.

―――――

What did you learn?

―――――

Describe a situation in which you would never use this strategy.

―――――

What would change if you got really good at Putting it on the table?

Notes:

Aim Your Control, Control Your Aim.

STRATEGY 4
Stop the action and regroup

Example

Mom spends an hour and a half helping Dale with her homework. She then asks Dale to take the clean laundry upstairs. Dale gets snotty, as if being asked to do that was unreasonable. Mom gets angry that Dale makes a big deal about such a little 'regular' request. Mom walks out and sits on the front porch to read, all the while thinking *She never appreciates anything I do for her*.

Mom sits there a few minutes plotting her revenge, *She'll be sorry. I will never again...* And feeling guilty, *What did I do wrong? Have I raised her to be this uncooperative?* Mom decides she won't go back in the house because *Dale needs to come out here...*

After about ten minutes, mom goes back in...
Mom: Now what?
Dale: I knew you'd come in.
Mom: I knew you wouldn't.
Dale: I would have eventually.
Mom: I knew that too.

Mom and Dale laugh. What could have turned into a huge fight becomes an insignificant interaction and brings them even closer as Dale says, "I've had a really bad day mom..." and goes on to share all. Mom, in turn, has the opportunity to share her feelings about gratitude and chores... Dale hears her and understands.

What might have turned this into a Great Divide?

- Instead of walking out to the front porch Mom could have stood there screaming at Dale for never doing anything around the house.

- Mom could have waited on the front porch for Dale to 'give in'.

- Mom could have walked back in angrily and dealt with Dale's ingratitude and her **automatic no** whenever she is asked to do something...

> **When we Stop the action and regroup we get to choose what 'winning' looks like.**

Section 4: Create the Reality

Strategy 4
Stop the action and regroup

Tips & Check In

✓ Write down the scenarios where you WILL remember to use this strategy.
(i.e. *When -THIS- happens, I will Stop the action and regroup.*)

✓ Have 3 sure-fired techniques to Stop the action ready at your fingertips.

✓ Plan your favorite regrouping techniques.
(Walking away, deep breathing, counting to 47, reminding yourself what's important, eating a big bowl of ice cream…)

When have you Stopped the action and regrouped?

―――※―――

What did this prevent?

―――※―――

When do you wish you would have Stopped the action and regrouped?

―――※―――

What helps you SLOW DOWN enough to put this strategy into action?

Notes:

STRATEGY 5

Lighten up

Example

Bob went to help his son Larry move some of the 'big stuff' from his dorm room. It had been Larry's last minute decision to get as much taken home as possible so the final move the following week would be easier. It also meant that Bob would be doing a lot of lugging up and down the stairs back at home because he'd be emptying the whole car himself. Bob didn't mind doing it at all.

Larry, however, had a secondary, unspoken, agenda. He wanted to be done by 2:00 so he could join his friends in the cafeteria. As Bob and Larry headed back to the room for another load, Bob heard Larry muttering what sounded like, "You're so slow. I can't believe how slowly you walk even when you're not carrying something heavy."

Bob could have gotten angry and felt taken advantage of. Bob could have said, "Don't you dare criticize me after all I'm doing for you, after all I always do for you." Bob could have escalated it into a big negative cycle to get the message across.

Instead Bob said, "Larry, I can barely hear you but I am absolutely sure you are talking about what a wonderful father you have and how much you appreciate his doing this with you."

Larry snickered, gave Bob a loving "got-it-dad" shove, and they continued in harmony... crisis averted.

**Conflict and tension are not always necessary
to get our messages across.**

**When we lighten up
we show our kids how to keep things in perspective.
We teach our kids that not everything is of equal weight.**

Section 4: Create the Reality

To Lighten Up

- ➤ To reduce the load, cut yourself and your kids some slack
- ➤ To loosen the grip on your agenda
- ➤ To make your suggestions without being so attached to how they are received
- ➤ To step back and not take everything quite so to-heart
- ➤ **TO REMEMBER TO TRULY ENJOY YOUR KIDS!**

FAQ: But what about when my son is being rude and non-compliant. Don't I need to show him who the boss is?

When your son is being rude or challenging and pulls you into a power struggle or when he has you responding angrily, who do you suppose is in charge? (Please forgive the sarcasm…)

When kids are being non-compliant or challenging, they are often struggling for control. Our task is to give it to them in a way that allows them to hear us and learn from us by clearly communicating our expectations, feedback, and concerns.
Remembering to Lighten up can help us do this.

Strategy 5
Lighten up

Tips & Check In

✓ We are better able to take care of the serious business of parenting when we are not taking ourselves quite so seriously.

✓ When we are angry, frustrated, or afraid, **Stopping the action and regrouping** allows us to decide if we need to Lighten up.

✓ Our kids can help us remember to Lighten up.
(Refer to Strategy 16, **Co-design**)

What helps you Lighten up?

———⸎———

When is it hard to Lighten up?

———⸎———

When do you wish you could Lighten up more?

———⸎———

What do you need to do to make that happen?

Notes:

Section 4: Create the Reality

STRATEGY 6

Let it go

Example

16-year-old Lenny is always complaining about the MONEY SITUATION … He's tired of not having all the things his friends have… He's tired of dad saying no "every time I want to buy something".

Dad has tried a number of ways to help Lenny understand the MONEY SITUATION. What the difficulties are… what he and mom are trying to do… what some of their fears are…

Heaven knows dad has tried to **Put it on the table**!

Lenny doesn't want to hear it… he can't be open right now to even considering it. Lenny just wants what his friends have.

To Consider

Dad has a couple of options:

1) To keep explaining and continue trying to help Lenny understand so it is easier for Lenny (and for mom and dad).

2) To get angry with Lenny for ignoring the facts and being close-minded and self-centered.

3) To accept the way Lenny feels and when Lenny asks for money simply give the answer dad feels is best. Dad could stop feeling responsible for trying to *make* Lenny understand. Dad could recognize that when Lenny is ready, if ever, dad will have the opportunity to teach the lesson.

**Let It Go is an alternative to
trying to crash through those Chronic Brick Walls…
(For other alternatives, refer to Section 6)**

**When we are standing in the Reality
we can decide what's worth holding on to and
what makes sense to let go of.**

Strategy 6
Let it go

Tips & Check In

✓ Identify an on-going struggle between you and your kids.

✓ Decide what you want to do about it by listing the pros and cons of Letting it go.

✓ Let it go does not have to be an Either-Or. There are often pieces we can let go of while holding on to the parts that really matter.

Looking back, when do you wish you would have Let it go?

―――◆―――

Looking forward, under what circumstances do you want to work on Letting it go?

―――◆―――

Under what circumstances is Letting it go not even an option?

―――◆―――

Given those circumstances, are there parts you can shift to achieve what it is you want?

Notes:

Section 4: Create the Reality

STRATEGY 7

Pull the plug on non-productive patterns

Example

While making a decision about what was best for her daughter Joan, Eileen tried to be fair. She tried to take into account where her 14-year-old daughter was coming from.

Joan: Why can't I go over to Laura's tonight?

As Eileen took a few seconds to weigh priorities, sort out her real reasons and reconsider her decision…

Joan jumped back in: See, you don't know. You don't care. That's why I hate this.

At that point, Eileen got flustered and started saying things that truly made no sense. And Eileen's confusing and contradictory statements validated all of Joan's complaints about her mom!

Identifying this as a typical communication pattern, Eileen recognized her valid need for space before responding when "Joan came at her". And she realized that each time she paused Joan immediately moved into that space with complaints and accusations and threw her off completely.

So Eileen began saying: Joan, you just asked me a question and I'd like to answer it. Give me a minute so I can figure out the best answer.

With this strategy, Eileen taught Joan…

Here's how I do things and here's why. My slowness is not a weakness. It is my wanting to be fair and wanting to do the best I can. It is my way of taking into account what's important to you.

Non-productive patterns are those repetitive interactions we keep having with our kids that always end in the same unsatisfying way.

> **Identifying unsuccessful patterns can be harder than changing them.**
>
> **Engage your kids in a non-productive pattern search by Putting it on the Table and asking Expansion Questions.**

Strategy 7
Pull the plug on non-productive patterns

Tips & Check In

✓ Identify two of your non-productive communication patterns.
- When I say this… My kids always…
- When my kids say this… I always…

✓ Identify two of your non-productive action patterns.
- When I do this… My kids always…
- When my kids do this… I always…

✓ Hold an A-ha Parenting conversation with your kids and invite them to be on the look-out for non-productive patterns.

✓ Remember, you can't see the non-productive patterns if you're not paying attention.

What perpetuates each of your non-productive patterns?

———❖———

How are you standing in the Illusion when they occur?

———❖———

What needs to shift in order to alter these patterns?

Notes:

Section 4: Create the Reality

STRATEGY 8

Assess the nag level

Longing to straighten up your daughter's room which feels like an invasion of privacy to her…

Itching to tell your son to go change that raggedy shirt knowing 'it's what all the kids are wearing…'

Wanting to give your daughter feedback on her new haircut…

Aching to suggest that your son stop slurping the soup…

- Sometimes these little urges go away by themselves.
- Sometimes giving in to them simply isn't worth the cost.
- Sometimes surrendering to them is cheap and feels really good.

> **When we rate our urges as High, Medium, Low on the Nag-O-Meter we can decide if they are worth indulging given the actual cost and the potential payoff.**

Strategy 8
Assess the nag level

Tips & Check In

✓ Make a list of your top 9 pet peeves.

✓ Decide which ones you want to address with your kids.

✓ Figure out a way to do that right up front by **Putting it on the table**.

✓ Decide which ones you want to stifle.

✓ For each one you want to stifle, find a way to **Let it go** so it doesn't use up a lot of your energy.

✓ Decide which ones you can't believe drive you crazy.

✓ Spend a lot of time laughing at those.

What would change if you got really good at Assessing the nag level?

―――◆―――

What do you suppose your kids would put on a list of their own top 9 peeves?

―――◆―――

How can you find out for sure?

Notes:

Section 4: Create the Reality

STRATEGY 9

Check in, check out

Example

Mom: You seem really upset. I assume you're angry at me because of what I said about your school work. Can we talk about that?

LuAnn: I'm not angry about that. You were right, I need to buckle down. It's just that I had a huge fight with Justine and I hate her.

Mom made an assumption. When she **Put it on the table**, she discovered that her assumption was incorrect and learned more about what was really going on.

> **CHECKING OUT our assumptions by CHECKING IN with our kids allows us to know what page they're on.**

Example

Celia: My kids are always fighting and I hate that.

Irma: Boy I know how annoying that can be.

Celia: Yeah, but it's more than that. It scares me.

Irma: What are you afraid of?

Celia: I want them to love and value each other and it scares me that they don't.

A-ha! Turns out Celia had this belief that fighting meant her kids didn't love and value each other. Up to this point this powerful and **unrecognized** assumption compelled Celia to try and stop the fighting every time because there was SO MUCH AT STAKE. Celia couldn't NOT try. And in addition to that all of her intervention attempts were based on this fear and as a result were extremely emotionally charged.

When Celia realized she held this underlying belief she was able to decide if it was true or not. She decided it wasn't.

For Celia, shining the light on this erroneous assumption gave her a lot more choice about whether or not to intervene when her kids were fighting. And when she chose to intervene she was able to do so in a much more effective manner.

> **CHECKING IN and recognizing our own APES allows us to CHECK OUT how much truth they really hold.**

Strategy 9
Check in, check out

Tips & Check In

✓ Just because we assume something is true doesn't make it so.

✓ Pay special attention to any conversations where both sides of the dialogue are taking place in your head.

✓ When in doubt check it out.

What will help you remember to check in with your kids
to make sure you are on the same page?

———◆———

How do you know when Checking in, checking out is needed?

———◆———

Describe three current situations that would be improved using this strategy.

Notes:

Section 4: Create the Reality

STRATEGY 10

Untangle the feelings

Example

> **Susan**: Mom, can I use your car tonight and bring it home tomorrow?
> **Mom**: Sure, I need to run some errands in the afternoon so call me in the morning and we'll make arrangements.

Susan calls the next morning…
> **Mom**: Go ahead and keep the car. I can either walk or ride my bike to the places I need to get to.

Susan chuckles and says, "Okay, bye."

Mom feels taken for granted since Susan didn't even acknowledge, let alone appreciate, (1) having the car and (2) what mom was willing to do so Susan could keep it.

Instead of just feeling the anger, letting it build up, mom **Puts it on the table**

> **Mom**: I had a hard time with our morning phone conversation. You showed no appreciation for how I rearranged my day so you could have the car. You didn't even say thanks.
>
> **Susan**: It just feels like I never have the car and that Tommy always has it.

Whew, it gets more complicated as Mom recognizes that THIS makes her really angry too. She finds herself thinking, *I'm not doing all this stuff for her anymore because it doesn't make a difference what I do… It only matters what I don't do.*

And then mom realizes that Susan is sharing her feelings, something mom wishes she would do more of…

When Susan returns the car:

> **Susan**: I'm sorry mom
> **Mom**: For what?

104

Aim Your Control, Control Your Aim.

Susan just shrugs her shoulders…

> **… and Mom says, meaning it**: I was thinking about how hard it must be to always feel like you're being cheated.

Instead of staying focused on her own feelings of being taken for granted, mom was able to shift her perspective, see beyond the immediate scenario, and acknowledge what was most important to Susan. As a result, mom encouraged Susan to share her feelings and both she and Susan learned more about themselves and each other.

> **When we recognize and take care of our own feelings we make more room for our kids' feelings.**

Section 4: Create the Reality

Strategy 10
Untangle the feelings

Tips & Check In

✓ There is a difference between anger and fear.

✓ Recognizing which is which (in both us and our kids) can be tough.

✓ Making the distinction is well worth the effort because being able to identify the difference is part of Untangling the feelings.

When do you get so overwhelmed by your own feelings
that you completely miss what's going on with your kids?

———◆———

Give an example when untangling your own feelings
helped you recognize your kids' feelings.

———◆———

How do your kids respond when you acknowledge their feelings?

———◆———

What makes you afraid?

———◆———

What makes you angry?

Notes:

STRATEGY 11

Word problems, go figure!

Example

Dad: It's hard for me when I see you being so self-centered.

Josh: I can't stand when you say that. I can't believe you called me self-centered again. I'm not self-centered. You don't know anything. I'm so sick of this.

Dad: What do you think the problem is?

Josh: I think it makes you really angry when I just think about what I want and when I forget that other people have feelings and schedules too.

Dad: Yeah Josh, that is what really bothers me.

Josh hated being called self-centered. As soon as dad used the term, Josh shut down and become defensive. When Josh defined the problem as he saw it however, it turned out that he and dad were talking about the same thing.

Words can bump up against all sorts of things like fears, insecurities, and hot buttons. We won't always choose the right words and some words our kids just need to hear…

But when we get a weird reaction, it's helpful to check out if there is a Word Problem involved.

Section 4: Create the Reality

Strategy 11
Word problems, go figure!

Tips & Check In

✓ We all have trigger words. Words that make us crazy. Words that hurt us. Words that scare us.

✓ We can discover the words and phrases that break down communication with our kids.

✓ We can **Clarify our Intentions** (A-ha 3:10) and find other ways to get our points across.

✓ We can engage our kids in this process.

How can you tell which words or phrases upset your kids?

―――◆―――

What words or phrases really push your buttons?

Hint: Consider what you hate being called, characterized as, or accused of.

―――◆―――

What do you and your kids have in common with respect to Word problems?

Notes:

STRATEGY 12

Explain the bottom line

Examples

Mom: I'd like you to check in each time you arrive in a new city.

Carol: I'm old enough to travel around Europe but I have to call my mommy every other day? That's bogus.

Mom: I get that it's irrational. But I'll sleep so much better knowing you've arrived safely to each destination. There's just so much going on right now. I wonder if, rather than doing this and resenting it, you could do it and know that you're helping me.
(See Strategy 17, **Reframe it**.)

Joey: I want the cookies.

Mom: No, you can have some later.

Joey: I want the cookies now.

Mom: No, you can't have them now. We need to be at the dentist in 10 minutes and there's no time for you to eat cookies and then brush your teeth.

Roy: Can I go out after the game with the rest of the team?

Dad: No, come straight home.

Roy: Okay

Dad Thinks: *I can't believe that Jimmy just got busted for drugs. Wonder who they'll put in for quarterback. I wonder what the rest of the team makes of this whole thing? I'm really freaked by all of this. I just need Roy home tonight...*

Sometimes Explaining the bottom line helps our kids accept it better. Sometimes an explanation is not necessary for helping our kids comply and accept.

Whether it's needed or not for acceptance however, each time we Explain the bottom line we give our kids more opportunities to learn about decision making and other people's perspectives.

> **Are you afraid your kids will always come to expect a reason?**
> **When it's not feasible to give one, explain why!**
> **Kids CAN learn to accept Bottom Lines both with and without...**

Section 4: Create the Reality

Strategy 12
Explain the bottom line

Tips & Check In

✓ To Explain the bottom line we need to know what the bottom line is and why we are drawing it.

✓ Sometimes the only way to explain it is to **Put our feelings on the table** and ask for our kids' understanding and trust. ("I'm not sure why I need you to do that but I know I really need you to. I get that a 'good' reason makes it easier to accept but I'd appreciate your doing it anyway.")

What helps you clarify your thoughts so you can
Explain the bottom line if you want to?

———◆———

How often don't you Explain the bottom line
because you think that as the parent you shouldn't have to?

———◆———

How can you **Lighten up** on "because I said so"?

———◆———

Do your kids know how to ask questions when they need more information?
(Section 6, **Avoiding Power Struggles,** might be helpful here.)

Notes:

Strategy 13

Stop trying to fix & solve, just listen

Example

Johnny: I hate school

Mom: Why?

Johnny: All the kids are dorks, the teachers don't know what they're talking about, I can't do long division, Kenny is mad at me, I lost my science book, I made the final out, I dropped my lunch tray, I have too much homework, Leslie laughed at my shoes…

It can be so easy to get overwhelmed with all the 'problems' we want to help our kids solve. It's a great relief when we realize we don't have to solve them all!

Sometimes all we can do is listen and commiserate.

> **Sometimes our kids just need:**
> **To vent and get it all out in the open.**
> **To know they can come to us with anything.**
> **To talk in order to arrive at their own conclusions or solutions.**

If you haven't worked much with this strategy, practice it A LOT. When you get really good at it, you will be amazed what a relief it is to know you don't have to have all the answers…

And keep in mind that when you are giving explanations you are indeed trying to **fix** the confusion and **solve** the misunderstanding… Remember this so you can choose when to **Explain the bottom line** (or anything else).

Section 4: Create the Reality

Strategy 13
Stop trying to fix and solve, just listen

Tips & Check In

✓ Fear, haste, and the uncontrollable need to be in charge can wreak havoc with this strategy.

✓ Selectively taking off our CEO hats is unbelievably freeing.

✓ Practice taking off that hat and notice how the world still keeps spinning...

How does it feel when someone really listens to YOU without jumping in?

―――◈―――

What helps you successfully Just Listen?

―――◈―――

How does being listened to affect your kids?

―――◈―――

What are the benefits of listening?

―――◈―――

When is it especially hard to not jump right in to fixing and solving?

Hint: Check in to see what underlying APES are there and if they are true. Look for your Catch 22s.

―――◈―――

What will make it easier for you to accept not having all the answers?

―――◈―――

How will you know when it's time to Just listen?

Notes:

STRATEGY 14

Just love 'em

Example

Susan was having a heck of a time helping her 28-year-old daughter plan her wedding. For nine months they engaged in long distance questioning, arguing, and disagreeing.

Susan was heading out to Santa Fe to finalize the arrangements. She was worried about how the visit would go given the last several months of phone calls. She asked what she should do.

The **PocketCoach** made a simple suggestion…. Drop the agenda… Forget about the To Do List… Just go out there and love her…

Susan came back glowing and raving about what a wonderful space just loving her daughter created. It was a fabulous trip and she and her daughter were able to take care of all the final arrangements.

> **Sometimes the best way to take care of business is to stop trying to take care of business.**

Example

Dad: Quit running around acting crazy.

Dad: I said, quit running around and acting crazy.

Dad: You're driving me nuts. Quit running around like a wild person.

Dad: I want you to go to your room.

Dad: I'm losing it here. I need you to settle down.

Dad: C'mere you goof. I gotta wrap you in a big old bear hug…

> **When it feels like we've simply run out of options, rather than getting frustrated and angry, we CAN choose to remember that this baffling child is ours to love as well as to train.**

Section 4: Create the Reality

FAQ: How do I know when to take care of business and when to Just love 'em?

As with most of parenting it's a judgment call. The more you shift towards Intentional Self, Lighten up, and know your kids, the more you will come to trust your own judgment.

Two things to keep in mind

1. When our kids are young, we have so much opportunity to teach them and to take care of business. They are with us most of the time. They want our energy and attention.

As they grow older and move away from us it's easy to feel an urgency to grab every possible moment together to take care of business.

So every opportunity we have we are teaching, advising… and driving them crazy! They resist, shut down, and avoid us even more which affords us even less opportunity to take care of business.

This is definitely a **Non-productive pattern** we need to **pull the plug on**.

2. When there is a crisis and when we or our kids are in a heightened state of emotion, it's easy to begin feeling "I only have one shot at this" so here goes…

We cram in all the lessons and instructions we can and what's likely to happen:

We overwhelm our kids. We make them angry. They feel we are trying to control them. We scare them. We accept all the responsibility of solving the problem at hand.

We get so lost in our **Catch 22** and so set in our agenda that there is no room for them, no room for us to hear them, see them, or learn what they need from us.

In short, we make matters worse.

This is when we need to **Stop the action and regroup** in order to ask ourselves, "Is this one of those times, right now, when I should Just love 'em?"

Strategy 14
Just love 'em

Tips & Check In

✓ With all the juggling we do to keep all the balls in the air, it can be easy to forget to show our kids how much we love 'em.

✓ We can mix Just love 'em in with taking care of business. These do not have to be mutually exclusive.

✓ For one hour each day, have your whole purpose be to Just love 'em.

When do you feel most compelled to take care of business with your kids?

———◆———

Under what circumstances do you wish you could take a step back
(take off that CEO hat) and Just love 'em?

———◆———

What stops you?

———◆———

How do you respond in a crisis?

———◆———

What helps you stay centered and grounded?

———◆———

What would improve if this strategy became an integral part of your parenting?

Notes:

Section 4: Create the Reality

STRATEGY 15

The butterfly & the bull

A Story

Katie is in the other room watching the news. She calls out to me, "Ron Santo is having his lower leg amputated". I know this is due to his diabetes. And I know Katie knows this.

I know at a gut level the impact this is probably having on her. I want to rush in there and talk about it. I want to point out the difference between her and Santo. I want her to share her fears with me.

But I don't. Katie has taught me how not to make a big deal of everything. She has taught me that when I do she shuts down. So I simply acknowledge how awful and wait to see if she wants to talk more about it... I have to follow Katie's lead...

Out of our fear, our love, and our wanting to help we sometimes ram ourselves down our kids' throats. Using a Butterfly Touch is often a whole lot more effective than acting like a Bull in a China Shop!

Caution:

The more our kids let us in or the greater our fear is the more likely we are to get reckless.

The more likely we are to shift to the Bull and go much farther than our kids need or are ready for.

Strategy 15
The butterfly and the bull

Tips & Check In

✓ Seeing our kids as separate and unique individuals helps us make a distinction between the butterfly and the bull.

✓ Slowing down (not being so quick to react) helps us assess situations and determine what is called for.

Give three examples when you have used the butterfly touch.

———◆———

How did you know to use it?

———◆———

Give three examples when you have gone way too far.

———◆———

How could you have avoided the bull for each of these?

Notes:

Section 4: Create the Reality

STRATEGY 16

Co-design

Co-design means to problem-solve, plan, and conspire with our kids.

Examples

Dad: I know you're frustrated at school right now. I'm not always sure when you come home to tell me about it if I am supposed to just listen or if it's okay for me to ask questions so I understand better. And sometimes I make suggestions that make you mad. Is there a way you can let me know right up front what you need from me when you walk in the door?

> **Allowing kids to Co-design the roles we play for them improves communication in a big way.**

Mom: The bedtime fights are really tiring, aren't they? Bedtime is 9:00 p.m. on school nights. What can we do to have the day end on an easier note? Do you want me to let you know when it's time to take your bath? Brush your teeth? Turn out the lights? Do you think posting a schedule might help?

> **Pre-planning ahead of time with our kids, when we're not in the throes of battle, makes it easier for our kids to accept the plans.**

Dad: When we get to grandma's it's important that you not make a lot of noise because she's not feeling well. How can I help you remember that? What would you like me to do when it's getting too loud for her?

> **Feedback is much better received when our kids help determine the shape of it.**

Strategy 16
Co-design

Tips & Check In

✓ Think in terms of engaging rather than overpowering.

✓ Every child can participate in Co-designing at some level if we allow them to.

Identify a topic around which you keep locking horns with your kids.
Describe how you could work together to devise a plan for rectifying the situation.
Start Co-designing…

How else would Co-designing come in handy?

What makes Co-designing hard for you?

What do you need to let go of in order to make Co-designing a viable option?

How are you already Co-designing with your kids?

Notes:

Section 4: Create the Reality

STRATEGY 17

Reframe it

Reframe means to revise, to alter, or to shift.

- We can reframe our APES (how we look at things) as well as the words we use (how we express ourselves).

- We use **Reframe it** to shape behavior, to build in success, and to shift the energy.

- When we **Reframe it**, we put a different spin on things for both ourselves and our kids.

Examples

The Scene: Your daughter is making one poor decision after another.

The Original: *I am stuck. I can't do this. I don't know how to help her. I don't know where to start. I am overwhelmed...*

The Reframe: *She is having a really tough time right now. She has so much more going on than I thought. I wonder how overwhelmed and stuck she feels...*

> **Shifting our perspective to what our kids might be feeling puts us in a better position to see how to help.**

The Scene: Your son is angry that you interfered and he's screaming at you.

The Original: You yell back at him, "Stop yelling at me."

The Reframe: You calmly say, "I get how important it is to you that I understand this. If you lower your voice a little I think it'll be easier for me to hear you."

> **By expressing a revised interpretation we give our kids something else to consider.**

Aim Your Control, Control Your Aim.

The Scene: Highway 65 at 5:00 pm; a car cuts into your lane, barely a yard ahead of you.

The Original: You find yourself in the throes of Road Rage. You feel your blood pressure rise. *That so-and-so... He should fry for that kind of driving. I hate when people do that to me.* And meanwhile, you're doing all you can not to ram his rear bumper.

The Reframe: *Boy is he in a hurry. I wonder how much of his life is spent rushing around, missing out on all the good stuff. It must feel awful to be that impatient. I think people like that must be really unhappy.* So you decide to bring some sunshine into his life and acknowledge his sudden presence with a smile and a wave!

> **By revising our understanding of a situation, we are better able to refrain from actions that will escalate matters whether it has to do with traffic or our kids!**

The Scene: Daily after school routine

The Original: For three weeks, Johnny walked in the house and mom told him to hang up his coat. And each day Johnny tossed his coat on the couch and headed to the kitchen for a snack. For three weeks, mom grew more and more frustrated and got snippier and snippier with Johnny for not listening and not follow simple directions. Mom grounded him for a week so he'd learn.

The Reframe: At 3:30 on Monday of the forth week, Johnny walked in and mom said, "Why don't you go have a snack". Johnny followed directions.

> **By changing our directions to match our kids' actions we get less frustrated and we might be able to find a different way to engage them.**

Section 4: Create the Reality

The Scene: You are at the grocery store with your 5-year-old who is whining for a candy bar

The Original: *He's trying to embarrass me into getting his own way. He is so spoiled. He does this all the time. I hate when he does this.*

The Reframe: *Boy he's testing the limits… hard to deal with but a very necessary part of his growing up.*

> **By not taking it all so personally
> we are better able to stand in the Reality.**

The Scene: Your daughter announces she doesn't want to live at home anymore.

The Original: "You have to decide what you want, what you are doing. You must figure out what you are going to live on."

The Reframe: "I have a feeling you're trying to figure out a lot of things right now. Is there any way I can help?"

> **By choosing words that are less confrontational
> we plant the seeds where they are more likely to grow.**

Strategy 17
Reframe it

Tips & Check In

✓ To Reframe it we need to be aware of how we are framing 'it' in the first place.

✓ To Reframe it we need to loosen our grip on our beliefs and agendas.

✓ To match our instructions to fit the kid-action we need to **Lighten up** and keep the big picture in mind.

Give three examples of how your assumptions and expectations
affect what you see and do.

―――◆―――

How could you reframe your most difficult Either-Or APES
to make things easier on you and/or your kids?

―――◆―――

Give 39 examples of how you help your kids Reframe it by showing them different perspectives.

Notes:

Section 4: Create the Reality

STRATEGY 18

Use the back door

The direct approach is not always the most effective approach. Especially after the fifth attempt!

The Front Door: "Get a job."

The Back Door: Stop giving him money for DVDs and clothes.

The Front Door: You are tired of your daughter's rudeness. You are tired of telling her to stop talking to you that way.

The Back Door: Give her a hug every time she is pleasant.

The Front Door: "Quit fighting. Quit fighting. Quit fighting. Quit fighting."

The Back Door: "Go in the bedroom and don't come out until you've figured out (**co-designed**) a plan to get along."

The Front Door: Grounding him four weekends in a row for coming in after his curfew.

The Back Door: Have him create a Power Point presentation to demonstrate how he would address the curfew issue.

The Front Door: "Pick up your toys and put them in the toy box. I said pick up your toys and put them… I said pick up your toys… I said…"

The Back Door: At the end of the day, impound all the left-laying-around-toys and have your kids develop a plan to earn them back.

If you are worried about being "manipulative, devious, and underhanded", **Reframe it**. Shift your perspective to "creative, flexible, and silly"!

> **A-ha Parenting includes subtlety and flair.**
> **So if the front door is locked, look for a back door.**

Strategy 18
Use the back door

Tips & Strategies

✓ The only way to **GUARANTEE** something will change is if we change something ourselves.

Describe a situation when the Back Door would have been a better entry point than continuing to bang (your head) on the Front Door?

———✣———

Identify the circumstances where you tend to get so caught up in your own agenda that the possibility of a Back Door doesn't even exist.

———✣———

Write down 5 Front Door/Back Door examples from your own parenting.

Notes:

Section 4: Create the Reality

STRATEGY 19

You're right, I can't make you

Example

Mom: Please go change those pants. They're way too tight.

Sally: All the kids are wearing them like this.

Mom: That's okay; I just don't think they're appropriate for school.

Sally: You can't make me change them.

Mom: You're right, I can't make you. So I'm hoping you'll change them because they bother me and I am asking you to change them.

When we admit that we can't make our kids do something, when we **Put that right on the table**, we diffuse their need to prove it.

> **In court, when the Prosecutor says,
> "We stipulate to that piece of evidence"
> the Defense Attorney doesn't have to waste time
> proving what everyone already knows.**

Strategy 19
You're right, I can't make you

Tips & Check In

✓ Kids can spend an awful lot of timing 'proving' that we "can't make them".

✓ Read Section 5, **Purposeful Structure**, to help you understand the difference between "making" your kids do something and providing the structure that maximizes the likelihood they will do it.

What makes it hard to admit "I can't make you"?

———◆———

What are you afraid might happen if you admit it?

———◆———

What might make it easier to admit it to your kids?

———◆———

What would make it easier to admit it to yourself?

———◆———

When is "**I CAN make you**" a true statement?

Notes:

Section 4: Create the Reality

STRATEGY 20

Turn off the automatic no

Examples

- Mom is it okay if I...? **No**
- Dad, can I have...? **No**
- Hey mom, some of the kids are... **No**

When you are busy or unaware, do you find yourself saying no even before your child is finished asking the question?

We can let our kids' requests be reminders to slow down long enough to hear the whole thing in order to consider our answers. When we hear them out, our kids won't be as likely to come back with, "That's what you always say".

**And if that is their retort,
once we have taken the time to consider their request,
we can more easily Explain the bottom line.**

Strategy 20
Turn off the automatic no

Tips & Check In

✓ Our Automatic no is often a product of habit and/or rushing around.

✓ Each time you hear yourself saying no, **Check in** to **Check out** if it was an automatic no or a thoughtful, intentional no.

✓ If it was automatic and you wish you hadn't said no so quickly, go ahead and change your mind by **Putting it on the table**, telling your kids what just occurred. (i.e. "Sometimes I say no before I really take the time to consider…")

Which kid requests trigger your automatic no?

Which of your kids tend to trigger your automatic no?

Describe the benefits of Turning off your automatic no.

Do your kids have an automatic no?

Is it a reflection of yours?

Do you have an automatic yes?

What triggers that?

Notes:

Section 4: Create the Reality

STRATEGY 21

Unscramble the issues

Step 1: Fill out the four quadrants.
Step 2: Invite your kids to fill them out.
Step 3: Set up an appointment that's convenient for both of you.
Step 4: Co-design a strategy for what needs to happen next.

We're On the Same Page	We Need to Explore & Clarify
Things both my kids and I want ME to be in charge of…	**Things I want to be in charge of but my kids want to be in charge of…**
Things both my kids and I want MY KIDS to be in charge of…	**Things I want my kids to be in charge of but they want me to be in charge of…**

Strategy 21
Unscramble the issues

Tips & Check In

✓ Scrambled issues involve ambiguity, uncertainty and vagueness.

✓ Scrambled issues lead to no-win situations for everyone involved.

✓ To unscramble the issues you have to recognize which ones are scrambled.

✓ Look for scrambled issues by identifying where you or your kids are confused, off balance, or feel out of sync.

✓ Anger could indicate scrambled issues. It could also indicate lack of acceptance around issues that are perfectly clear. Recognize the difference…

List ten things that would change if you unscrambled
the control and responsibility issues in your family.

Identify three other issues that you could unscramble using the quadrants.

Ask your kids what issues they think are scrambled.

What are the real benefits of getting good at Unscrambling the issues?

Notes:

Section 4: Create the Reality

STRATEGY 22

Walk 13 steps in their Nikes

Step 1:

You: My boss is driving me crazy... He's always... I never get to...

Your Hairdresser: Write a letter to the president of the company. Quit your job. Stand up for yourself. Apply for her position. Don't let it bother you. Quit bucking the system. Just do what she tells you to do.

How does it feel when you just want to vent a little and someone with all the answers tells you how to fix it?

Step 2:

Your Wife: Would you like to have steak, pork chops, or chicken for dinner?

You: Chicken

Your Wife: Sorry, we don't have any. We're having steak.

How does it feel when someone gives you options and choices but there is really only one right answer?

Step 3:

You: I just got the promotion of a lifetime.

Your Husband: Does that mean we're going to have to move? We'll have to get the kids' school files transferred. How should we invest the extra income? How much more time will that mean at the office?

How does it feel when, instead of celebrating your moment, the whole focus is on taking care of business or why it won't work?

Step 4:

You: So I stopped at my moms and she said... And I got nervous and said... and she didn't understand where I was coming from so she asked...

Your Friend: What time is your next appointment?

How does it feel when your lips are moving and no one notices you are trying to tell them something?

Aim Your Control, Control Your Aim.

Step 5:

Your Co-worker walks in 45 minutes late and says: You look great. What are you going to order for lunch?

How does it feel when other people don't apologize when they should?

Step 6:

You: I don't want to talk about it.

Your Father: So what's this all about?

You: I really don't want to talk about it.

Your Father: Okay, but did something happen at work today?

How does it feel when someone tries to push you into sharing when you are not ready?

Step 7:

Your Insurance Agent: Fax me your A-26XY0PGF Form right away.

You: I don't understand what you're asking.

Your Insurance Agent: I need the A-26 XY0PGF Form immediately to process the claim.

You: I don't know what that is.

Your Insurance Agent: It's in your B-381TwoF Manual and I can't do anything without that form!

How does it feel when people won't take the time to answer your questions in a way that helps you understand?

Step 8:

6:30 a.m. Your Mother: Well hi. It's beautiful outside. What a great day. I just got back from… and I saw… Have you heard from your brother? What are you going to do today? Did you hear about Mr. Miller?

You: Ugh…

How does it feel when someone doesn't respect your "I'm not a Morning Person" Status.

Step 9:

Your Significant Other: Saturday night we're having dinner with the Smith's and then going to Sue's party. We'll stop and pick up a bottle of wine and some flowers. Wear that new blue sweater your mom bought you…

How does it feel when someone is always telling rather than asking?

Section 4: Create the Reality

Step 10:

    You: I've decided to go back to school for my MBA.

    Your Sister: You were never a very good student. Remember how hard the math classes were? You always hated school. Why would you want to do that?

How does it feel when the people you care about don't seem to believe in you?

Step 11:

    You: It doesn't feel like we really talk anymore.

    Your Spouse: What do you mean?

    You: It seems like all we ever talk about is the kids and money.

    Your Spouse: But all that's so important.

    You: I know. But what about us and our relationship?

    Your Spouse: Okay, we'll plan a trip to Cancun next July. Just the two of us, no kids and the heck with what it'll cost. We'll have a whole week to talk.

How does it feel when people turn a simple, immediate solution into a big, far away one?

Step 12:

    You: I'm going to tear down the garage and build a sweat lodge.

    Your Son: Dad, what will the neighbors think? What will my friends say?

How does it feel when those close to you worry more about what other people think than what you think?

Step 13:

    You: Why are we withdrawing our three million dollar proposal?

    Your Boss: Because I said so!

How does THAT feel?

> We can't ALWAYS put ourselves in our kids' shoes…
> …but it never hurts to try.

Aim Your Control, Control Your Aim.

Strategy 22
Walk 13 steps in their Nikes

Tips & Check In

✓ Pay attention to the things that hurt your feelings or make you angry.

✓ Notice if you do any of these same things with other people.

✓ Share this Strategy (pages 132 - 134) with your kids. Ask them which ones apply.

✓ Laugh about all of it and then together decide what needs to change.

Which of the thirteen steps have your name written all over them?

———◈———

What do you do that bothers your kids?

———◈———

Which ones do you want to do something about?

———◈———

How do you help your kids Walk 13 steps in someone else's Nikes?

———◈———

What helps you remember what it felt like to be a kid?

Notes:

Section 4: Create the Reality

STRATEGY 23

Think smaller

Example

Jean missed the relationship she once had with her 16-year-old daughter. So she decided to spend one weekend a month at a hotel with her daughter to work on the three R's... relaxing, reminiscing, and reconnecting.

The trick was following through on the plan. Schedules, competing priorities, and her daughter's social life kept getting in the way.

Jean discovered other things she could do:

1. She began sitting at the counter while her daughter ate her after-school snack.
2. She invited her daughter to peel the potatoes for dinner.
3. She got her daughter to **co-design** a two-week moratorium on TV between dinner and bedtime three nights a week.
4. She started sharing the highlights of her day with her daughter.
5. She put love notes in her daughter's backpack.

> **So often it's the little day-to-day things we do that make the big difference...**

(Refer to **Shifts: Moving Along Our Continuums A-ha 3:6**, pg. 61, to reinforce this strategy.)

Strategy 23
Think smaller

Tips & Check In

✓ Choose one of your A-ha Parenting goals.

✓ List ten things you could do on a monthly basis to move closer towards this goal.

✓ Now Think smaller and name six things you could do on a weekly basis.

✓ Now get really tiny and identify one thing you could do or say each morning and evening that would move you closer to your goal.

How do you distinguish between 'big' and 'small'?

―――◆―――

What changes when you Think smaller?

Notes:

Section 4: Create the Reality

STRATEGY 24

Hang in there

Example

For three years Jason had been immersed in his business. So much so that he barely had time for anything else. He left the house before his son woke up and got home with a briefcase full of work to do twelve hours later...

A mild heart attack compelled Jason to rethink his priorities, to make choices based on what was truly important to him. So he decided to pay more attention to his son.

But every time he tried to engage him in a conversation the 13-year-old had other places he wanted to be and other things he needed to do.

Jason got discouraged...

Another Example

Stan, who we met in **Parents Along the Way**, discovered the power of shifting towards Intentional Self and providing clear limits for his kids. But his darn kids kept behaving the same way. In fact, their behavior got worse.

(**Note:** A tried and true behavior modification principle: When we 'tighten up' on inappropriate behavior, the inappropriate behavior will initially increase in intensity and frequency.)

Stan was perplexed, *I'm doing what I need to, why aren't my kids responding the 'right' way?*

We notice something that we'd like to shift or change. Perhaps we want to be more open to our kids' viewpoints, demonstrate our love more overtly, or provide more limits and structure. We try some new strategies.

And one of our expectations (APES) is that our kids will instantly notice the change and respond immediately.

As you've undoubtedly noticed, it doesn't always work that way. Kids will test. Kids have to learn to trust new behaviors and patterns. Kids have to figure out what all of it means to them.

> **Kids will adjust, or not, in their own way, according to their own time frame.**
> **(Refer to A-ha 3:9, Curb Your Impatience.)**

Strategy 24
Hang in there

Tips & Check In

✓ It can be difficult to differentiate between Hanging in there effectively and not taking the action (making the changes) you need to for the sake of your kids.

✓ Hanging in there is a conscious choice, not a habit born out of unawareness.

✓ Without making yourself crazy, **Check in, check out** what doesn't seem to be working right now and decide if Hanging in there is the right choice.

✓ Trust your decision and maintain awareness.

Describe three times you successfully hung in there and were satisfied with the results.

―――◊―――

When is it hardest for you to Hang in there?

―――◊―――

What helps you Hang in there?

―――◊―――

What are you trying to Hang in there with right now?

―――◊―――

What support do you need?

―――◊―――

How can you ask for it?

Notes:

Section 4: Create the Reality

STRATEGY 25

Aim your control...Control your aim

A Story

I hadn't heard from Katie yet... Sarah had traveled to Paris and I didn't know where she was staying... My only shower drain was clogged up... There was way too much I wanted to include in the two-day workshop...

Yup, my trusty side-kick *Under-Control* had turned into her alter-ego the Nine-Headed Hydra *Out-of-Control* and was devouring everything in sight...

I was waking up an hour and a half before the alarm... I had five times the usual number of messages clogging up my Inbox... I couldn't keep up with the weeds...

I could not sit still... I couldn't NOT sit still... The house was the pits... The brakes needed fixing which would cost an arm and a leg... I was even cynical about my saintly neighbor's motives... I hated it!

Coming from Intentional Self, I knew that barking out directives to my staff and advising the Plumber on how to live a meaningful life, no matter how tempting *that* was, would not bring the order and predictability I craved.

What I needed was to...

    Recognize the silliness
    Exercise
    Meditate
    Eat a huge salad with lots of different vegetables
    Make a list
    Begin writing
    Enjoy the current novel
    Relax in a hot tub

                         ...REMEMBER what works for me.

Aim Your Control, Control Your Aim.

FAQ: Wait a minute. I know I need to make sure my home, my family, is not out-of-control, not chaotic. How will soaking in the tub accomplish that?

As we have discovered, the best way to keep things from spinning out-of-control is by not spinning out-of-control ourselves. Being grounded and centered enables us to shift towards the Reality and decide what we want for our kids and from our kids. Feeling in control of ourselves allows us to choose the messages we send and provide the limits and guidelines our kids need to keep chaos at a minimum.

Feeling in control of ourselves increases our Chaos Tolerance Level, the point at which we get swept up in the chaos. And this higher Chaos Tolerance Level makes it much less likely that we will escalate things if and when they do start.

"Serenity is not freedom from the storm,
but peace amid the storm."
- *unknown* -

Section 4: Create the Reality

Strategy 25
Aim your control...Control your aim

Tips & Check In

- ✓ We can do things to minimize both the intensity and the frequency of feeling like we are spinning out-of-control.
- ✓ The earlier we sense the spinning and do something to slow it down the easier it is to stop the spinning.

Prevention:

- ✓ List 10 ways to increase the amount of peace and serenity in your life.
- ✓ List 10 ways to prevent that out-of-control feeling in the first place.
- ✓ Notice how these two lists are similar and different.

Intervention:

- ✓ List 5 ways to get organized when you feel out-of-control.
- ✓ List 5 ways to reintroduce predictability when you feel out-of-control.
- ✓ Notice how these two lists are similar and different.

When do you spin out-of-control?

What is your typical response?

How can you tell when the spinning has begun?

Notes:

Aim Your Control, Control Your Aim.

Strategy Check List

Strategy 1
Shift to a Learning Stance

☐ Got it!   ☐ I love it   ☐ I hate it

☐ I need more reflection on it   ☐ I need more practice with it

☐ It maximizes my sense of control by _____

☐ It maximizes my kids' sense of control by _____

Strategy 2
Let them have it (the responsibility that is)

☐ Got it!   ☐ I love it   ☐ I hate it

☐ I need more reflection on it   ☐ I need more practice with it

☐ It maximizes my sense of control by _____

☐ It maximizes my kids' sense of control by _____

Strategy 3
Put it on the table

☐ Got it!   ☐ I love it   ☐ I hate it

☐ I need more reflection on it   ☐ I need more practice with it

☐ It maximizes my sense of control by _____

☐ It maximizes my kids' sense of control by _____

Section 4: Create the Reality

Strategy 4
Stop the action and regroup

☐ Got it! ☐ I love it ☐ I hate it

☐ I need more reflection on it ☐ I need more practice with it

☐ It maximizes my sense of control by _____

☐ It maximizes my kids' sense of control by _____

Strategy 5
Lighten up

☐ Got it! ☐ I love it ☐ I hate it

☐ I need more reflection on it ☐ I need more practice with it

☐ It maximizes my sense of control by _____

☐ It maximizes my kids' sense of control by _____

Strategy 6
Let it go

☐ Got it! ☐ I love it ☐ I hate it

☐ I need more reflection on it ☐ I need more practice with it

☐ It maximizes my sense of control by _____

☐ It maximizes my kids' sense of control by _____

Strategy 7
Pull the plug on non-productive patterns

☐ Got it! ☐ I love it ☐ I hate it

☐ I need more reflection on it ☐ I need more practice with it

☐ It maximizes my sense of control by _____

☐ It maximizes my kids' sense of control by _____

Aim Your Control, Control Your Aim.

Strategy 8
Assess the nag level

☐ Got it! ☐ I love it ☐ I hate it

☐ I need more reflection on it ☐ I need more practice with it

☐ It maximizes my sense of control by _____

☐ It maximizes my kids' sense of control by _____

Strategy 9
Check in, check out

☐ Got it! ☐ I love it ☐ I hate it

☐ I need more reflection on it ☐ I need more practice with it

☐ It maximizes my sense of control by _____

☐ It maximizes my kids' sense of control by _____

Strategy 10
Untangle the feelings

☐ Got it! ☐ I love it ☐ I hate it

☐ I need more reflection on it ☐ I need more practice with it

☐ It maximizes my sense of control by _____

☐ It maximizes my kids' sense of control by _____

Strategy 11
Word problems, go figure!

☐ Got it! ☐ I love it ☐ I hate it

☐ I need more reflection on it ☐ I need more practice with it

☐ It maximizes my sense of control by _____

☐ It maximizes my kids' sense of control by _____

Section 4: Create the Reality

Strategy 12
Explain the bottom line

☐ Got it! ☐ I love it ☐ I hate it

☐ I need more reflection on it ☐ I need more practice with it

☐ It maximizes my sense of control by _____

☐ It maximizes my kids' sense of control by _____

Strategy 13
Stop trying to fix & solve, just listen

☐ Got it! ☐ I love it ☐ I hate it

☐ I need more reflection on it ☐ I need more practice with it

☐ It maximizes my sense of control by _____

☐ It maximizes my kids' sense of control by _____

Strategy 14
Just love 'em

☐ Got it! ☐ I love it ☐ I hate it

☐ I need more reflection on it ☐ I need more practice with it

☐ It maximizes my sense of control by _____

☐ It maximizes my kids' sense of control by _____

Strategy 15
The butterfly and the bull

☐ Got it! ☐ I love it ☐ I hate it

☐ I need more reflection on it ☐ I need more practice with it

☐ It maximizes my sense of control by _____

☐ It maximizes my kids' sense of control by _____

Aim Your Control, Control Your Aim.

Strategy 16
Co-design

☐ Got it!   ☐ I love it   ☐ I hate it

☐ I need more reflection on it   ☐ I need more practice with it

☐ It maximizes my sense of control by _____

☐ It maximizes my kids' sense of control by _____

Strategy 17
Reframe it

☐ Got it!   ☐ I love it   ☐ I hate it

☐ I need more reflection on it   ☐ I need more practice with it

☐ It maximizes my sense of control by _____

☐ It maximizes my kids' sense of control by _____

Strategy 18
Use the back door

☐ Got it!   ☐ I love it   ☐ I hate it

☐ I need more reflection on it   ☐ I need more practice with it

☐ It maximizes my sense of control by _____

☐ It maximizes my kids' sense of control by _____

Strategy 19
You're right, I can't make you

☐ Got it!   ☐ I love it   ☐ I hate it

☐ I need more reflection on it   ☐ I need more practice with it

☐ It maximizes my sense of control by _____

☐ It maximizes my kids' sense of control by _____

Section 4: Create the Reality

Strategy 20
Turn off that automatic no

☐ Got it!   ☐ I love it   ☐ I hate it

☐ I need more reflection on it   ☐ I need more practice with it

☐ It maximizes my sense of control by _____

☐ It maximizes my kids' sense of control by _____

Strategy 21
Unscramble the issues

☐ Got it!   ☐ I love it   ☐ I hate it

☐ I need more reflection on it   ☐ I need more practice with it

☐ It maximizes my sense of control by _____

☐ It maximizes my kids' sense of control by _____

Strategy 22
Walk 13 steps in their Nikes

☐ Got it!   ☐ I love it   ☐ I hate it

☐ I need more reflection on it   ☐ I need more practice with it

☐ It maximizes my sense of control by _____

☐ It maximizes my kids' sense of control by _____

Strategy 23
Think smaller

☐ Got it!   ☐ I love it   ☐ I hate it

☐ I need more reflection on it   ☐ I need more practice with it

☐ It maximizes my sense of control by _____

☐ It maximizes my kids' sense of control by _____

Strategy 24
Hang in there

☐ Got it!   ☐ I love it   ☐ I hate it

☐ I need more reflection on it ☐ I need more practice with it

☐ It maximizes my sense of control by _____

☐ It maximizes my kids' sense of control by _____

Strategy 25
Aim your control... Control your aim

☐ Got it!   ☐ I love it   ☐ I hate it

☐ I need more reflection on it ☐ I need more practice with it

☐ It maximizes my sense of control by _____

☐ It maximizes my kids' sense of control by _____

What do these strategies have in common?

What do these strategies require of you?

Which strategies would you like to teach your kids?

Notes

We CAN get our kids to try new things when we help them discover compelling reasons to do so, when we invite rather than demand, and when we let go of some of our own "expertise" to make room for theirs…

Section 5

Purposeful Structure

We are an integral part of the structure we create for our kids.

Aim Your Control, Control Your Aim.

Section 5: Purposeful Structure

Managing Structure

As indicated in Section I, The Control Continuum Paradigm has three components: our kids, us, and the structure we provide. We are standing in the Reality when we focus on managing ourselves and the structure rather than on trying to control our kids.

This section explores what structure is and how to use it to meet our kids' needs.

Structure refers to the things we do, the steps we take, that modify the environment within which our kids live.

This includes all aspects of their environment: **physical, social, emotional, and intellectual.**

We provide structure (we modify our kids' environment) in order to*

- Shape behavior
- Develop values
- Teach lessons
- Maintain physical safety
- Extend emotional security
- Improve organization and memory

Purposeful Structure

Everything we say and don't say, do and don't to, impacts our kids' environment. **Purposeful Structure** is choosing HOW we will impact the environment in order to best meet our kids' needs. We provide Purposeful Structure by:

1. Working with the **Structure Continuum** to achieve the above objectives*

| Too Much Structure | Just Right | Too Little Structure |

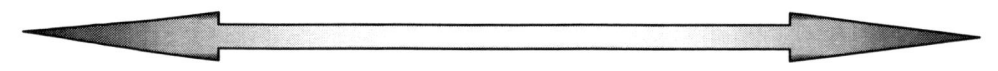

Note: Viewed as a continuum, we bust open the Either-Or APE, "Either the structure is working or it's not". As a continuum we have lots of places to look and tools to use to adjust the structure.

153

Section 5: Purposeful Structure

    2. Using the Primary Adjustment Tools to shift towards **Just Right**
        a. **The Feedback/Message Tool**
        b. **The Rules/Expectations Tool**
        c. **The Options Tool**
        d. **The Outcomes Tool**

We are providing the correct amount of structure for our kids (**Just Right**) when we have matched the level of **Purposeful Structure** to the amount of structure they need. In other words, we use the Primary Adjustment Tools to intentionally increase and decrease structure based upon what we believe our kids need.

Of course the complicated part is figuring out how much structure our kids need so we can use the Tools effectively.

Understanding "The Gray Area Factor" and "Internal Structure" gives us better insight into our kids' ever-changing need for structure.

- Give several examples of how you provide structure (modify the environment) for your kids.

- For each example, what was the basis for your decision to modify their environment in this way?

- What questions keep coming up or have you stumped about structure? (You'll come back to these questions at the end of this section.)

Aim Your Control, Control Your Aim.

A-ha 5:1

The Gray Area Factor

Life is full of complexity and uncertainty. We constantly find ourselves in situations in which the 'answers' aren't given, things aren't clear-cut, or the correct plan of action isn't immediately obvious.

What time should I get home so I'm not late for the PTA meeting? What do I feel like doing right now? Where am I supposed to be after work? What will I cook for dinner tonight? Is this boy good for my son to hang around with? What do I want to be when (if?) I grow up?

The **Gray Area Factor (GAF)** refers to the **amount of complexity and uncertainty** in any given situation.

The level of structure our kids need us to provide is determined by how much complexity and uncertainty is present and how prepared they are to independently deal with it.

Exercise 5:1

You already know about the Gray Area Factor. You just didn't have this name for it.

1. Using the Gray Area Preference Sheet on the next page, indicate your preference on each continuum.

2. Then return and answer these questions:

    - With respect to the GAF, how do the choices on the left-hand side of the sheet compare to those on the right-hand side?

    - What is required of you as you move along each preference continuum?

3. Describe the Gray Area Factor in your own words.

Section 5: Purposeful Structure

Gray Area Factor
Preference Sheet

Small Gathering of Friends ←——————————————→ Large Dinner Party

One Project ←——————————————→ Lots of Projects

A written to-do list ←——————————————→ Relying on memory for what to do

A Scheduled Day ←——————————————→ Free Time

1 Pair of Shoes ←——————————————→ 10 Pairs of Shoes

Direct Feedback ←——————————————→ Indirect Feedback

Knowing what's next ←——————————————→ Not knowing what's coming

| A-ha 5:2 |

Internal Structure

"The level of structure our kids need us to provide is determined by how much complexity and uncertainty is present and **how prepared they are to deal with it independently.**" (From the box on page 155)

Our kids' ability to deal with uncertainty and complexity depends on the development of their **Internal Structure**. Internal Structure is what enables our kids to make good decisions, problem-solve efficiently, and establish effective priorities. Internal Structure involves a sense of right and wrong, safe and unsafe.

Consider Internal Structure from an adult's point of view…

Examples

When the GAF feels too high, when there is too much complexity and uncertainty, it is our Internal Structure that has us:

- Making To-do lists
- Reprioritizing and learning to say no
- Establishing clear-cut time frames
- Shutting ourselves in the bedroom for 15 minutes

And when the GAF is too low…

- Painting the living room red
- Moving to Australia
- Trying that new Thai restaurant
- Taking a different route home from work

Purposeful Structure fills in the Gap…

…between the **Internal Structure** our kids bring to each situation and the total structure needed for them to successfully manage the **Gray Area Factor**.

Our ultimate goal as parents is to help our kids develop a strong Internal Structure so they can effectively deal with and thrive within an ever-increasing Gray Area Factor.

Section 5: Purposeful Structure

Picture It

Imagine a circle representing the structure required for our kids to manage the uncertainty and complexity of a situation. And our goal is to keep this circle filled to the max, to 100%[4].

**The Structure Required to Manage
The Uncertainty and Complexity (GAF)
of a Situation**

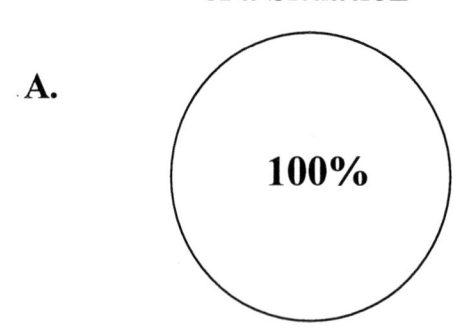

A.

100%

As our kids get older, they develop more **Internal Structure.** In order to maintain the hypothetical 100% we need to modify our responses and the amount of structure we provide. Our goal is to **fill the gap** between what our kids can and can't independently handle given the amount of uncertainty and complexity of a given situation.

As newborns, our kids are unable to provide any of the structure so we fill in the gap by providing 100%. At age two, they can perhaps provide 5%[5] through their Internal Structure so we cut back to 95%. By age 16, they might be up to 50% so we only need to provide 50% of the required structure, given the level of complexity and uncertainty.

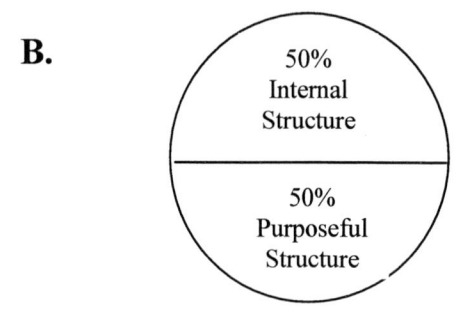

B.

50% Internal Structure

50% Purposeful Structure

Just Right for the 16-year-old

---

[4] In our dreams! 100% all the time is an unrealistic goal. We don't need to be perfect...
[5] Percentages are for illustration purposes only. Irma is not implying that she has a mathematical formula for measuring Internal and External Structure.

Aim Your Control, Control Your Aim.

Exercise 5:2

1. Describe five ways you have modified the structure for your kids that illustrate The Hypothetical 100% Principle

2. Describe five circumstances where you and your kids disagreed about how the 100% should break down.
   - If you didn't change your mind, describe why in terms of the GAF.
   - If you changed your mind, use the GAF to describe why.

From A-ha 2:1 The Obstacles and Fallacies at the Illusion End:

**"Kids are born to struggle for independence.
Standing in the Illusion, we are battling Mother Nature."**

It is our kids' developing Internal Structures
that make this statement true.

Section 5: Purposeful Structure

A-ha 5:3

Just Right

Here's how the **Gray Area Factor** looks on the **Structure Continuum**:

GAF Too Low	Just Right	GAF Too High
Too Much Structure		Too Little Structure

The structure is **Just Right** when our kids' **Internal Structure** and our **Purposeful Structure** equal the hypothetical 100%.

When we shift towards the middle of the continuum and the structure is **Just Right**, we are letting our kids deal with a healthy amount of uncertainty and complexity. In the middle, we have done an effective job assessing and being aware of what our kids can and can't handle. And we have provided the structure they need to successfully manage the situation.

Example

Sally tells her 5-year-old that he can only ride his bike to the end of the block. Going around the block and crossing streets involves more complexity and uncertainty than a 5-year-old is ready for. This rule provides the right level of structure given what her 5-year-old is capable of handling independently.

But Sally wouldn't dream of telling her 16-year-old daughter, "You can only drive the car to the end of the block and then you need to turn around." But she might instruct the new driver to stay off the expressways…

Important Note: 'Just Right' includes Room for Growth.

Our job as parents is to not rush in and cover the **whole** gap with our rules and limits. For our kids' Internal Structures to keep developing they need to experience some complexity and uncertainty beyond their current capability. Purposeful Structure includes this **Room for Growth**.

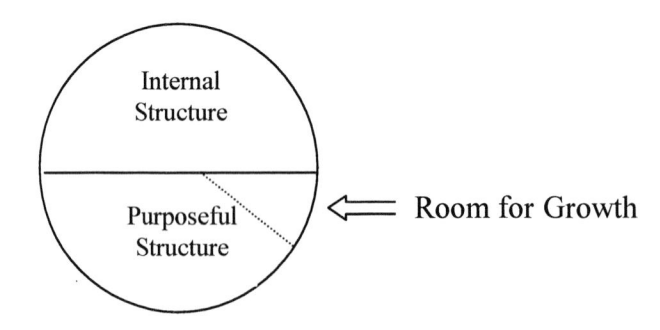

⇐ Room for Growth

Aim Your Control, Control Your Aim.

➤ Our role (our portion with respect to The Hypothetical 100% Principle) in **Just Right** changes **over time** as our kids develop more Internal Structure, as they get better at handling uncertainty and complexity on their own.

➤ Our role (our portion with respect to The Hypothetical 100% Principle) in **Just Right** changes **across circumstances** as the level of uncertainty and complexity shifts.

> **FAQ: How much Room for Growth do I leave in order to still be at Just Right?**
>
> Irma doesn't have a formula for this one either! Our decisions have to be based upon what we know about our kids. And at the risk of repeating this one too many times, our best shot at knowing our kids is two-fold: 1.) Standing in the Reality so they are not hiding from us and 2.) Coming from Intentional Self so we are paying attention to who they are and what they are capable of.
>
> Keep in mind too that the Create the Reality Strategies are most helpful for determining how much Room for Growth to leave…

Exercise 5:3

Let's see what **Just Right** feels like to you…

1. Identify three situations where you are most comfortable.

2. Describe each of these situations in terms of the GAF:
   The Gray Area Factor feels Just Right because…

3. Identify three situations where you are most uncomfortable.

4. Describe each of these situations in terms of the Gray Area Factor:
   The Gray Area Factor feels too high or too low because…

5. For each situation you listed in # 3, describe how you could adjust things to make the situation closer to **Just Right** for you.

Section 5: Purposeful Structure

A-ha 5:4

Too Little Structure

The Structure Continuum

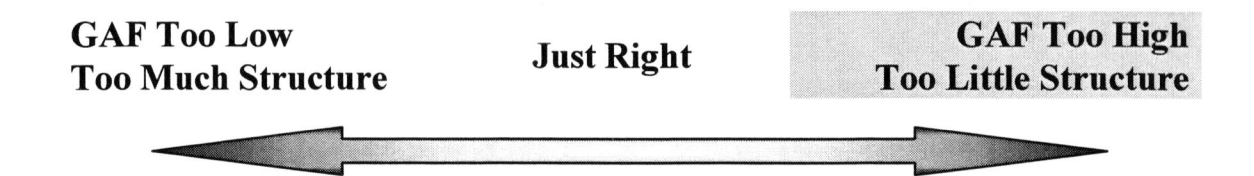

GAF Too Low	Just Right	GAF Too High
Too Much Structure		Too Little Structure

When there is too little structure we haven't made things clear enough or simplified them enough. Things still aren't as **black and white** as our kids need. Perhaps we:

- Overestimated our kids' **Internal Structure** or how much Room for Growth to leave.
- Underestimated the amount of uncertainty and complexity present.
- Weren't paying attention or didn't know what to do with the structure.

This will happen, probably a lot. We can use these experiences to get an even better understanding of the GAF and how to provide Purposeful Structure. All we can do is learn as we go and remember that we don't need to be perfect.

The experience of "GAF Too High, Too Little Structure"

There is more going on than we can cope with. There is too much open-endedness. We may feel like things are whirling out-of-control with all the stimulation, distractions, or risk. We feel uncomfortable, overwhelmed, stressed, and off-balance. We are less efficient. We doubt ourselves. Towards the right-hand side of the continuum, our decision-making process may be impaired.

An Adult Example

At weddings, I really dislike the stand-around-before-dinner time. I don't like having to choose where to stand, what to do with my hands, and who to talk with. Sitting down at my assigned table simplifies things for me, reduces the gap between the Gray Area Factor and how much complexity and uncertainty I feel comfortable with. Sitting at the table adds the structure I prefer in large social settings.

We know what it feels like when the GAF is too high (when there isn't enough structure). And this understanding gives us more insight into what our kids experience when we don't provide enough structure.

| A-ha 5:5 |

Too Much Structure

The Structure Continuum

GAF Too Low — **Just Right** — **GAF Too High**
Too Much Structure — **Too Little Structure**

With respect to The Hypothetical 100% Principle, when we provide too much structure (the total goes above 100%) we aren't requiring or allowing our kids to handle what they can. We aren't:

- Giving our kids the responsibilities they are prepared for.
- Acknowledging what they are capable of.
- Providing enough Room for Growth.
- Showing them the trust and respect they deserve as individuals.

The experience of "GAF Too Low, Too Much Structure"

On the left-hand side of the continuum, there isn't enough going on. There isn't enough stimulation or possibility. We may feel stifled, bored, stuck, or hemmed in. It may feel as if we have no options or that there is nothing to do. It may feel like there is nothing worth doing.

An Adult Example

Joe is tired of his job. It is always the same. Punch in at 8:30, work on the spreadsheets and balance the books, eat a peanut butter sandwich for lunch at 12:00, go back to the spreadsheets and books and punch out at 5:00[6]. Joe is looking forward to the new boss starting on Monday because it might shake things up a bit and increase the GAF.

Too much structure affects our kids this way too. Our job is to take into consideration how much excitement and risk they crave with how much we believe is good for them and how much they can successfully handle.

---

[6] And for some people, this degree of structure, this GAF level, feels **Just Right**. We need to know our kids…

Section 5: Purposeful Structure

> **The trick here is to remember that our kids are not us.
> We can't base our decisions strictly upon
> how much excitement, risk, chaos, and variety
> feels Just Right to us.**

Exercise 5:4/5

1. Describe your reaction when the GAF is too high for you.
   - How do you create more structure for yourself?
2. Describe your reaction when the GAF is too low for you.
   - How do you alter the structure to bring it back to Just Right?
3. Give three examples demonstrating how the structure your kids need from you has changed over time.
   - Describe these in terms of the GAF and your kids' Internal Structure.
4. Give three examples demonstrating how the structure your kids need from you has changed under different circumstances.
   - Describe these in terms off the GAF and their Internal Structure.
5. Summarize what's critical for you to remember about Too Much Structure, Too Little Structure, and Just Right.

Aim Your Control, Control Your Aim.

FAQ: I still don't get it completely. Why not just talk about increasing and decreasing structure based on what my kids can and can't handle? Why bother with this whole Gray Area Factor business?

The GAF helps "Unscramble the Issues"
(Strategy 21)

Your son isn't getting his homework done. I could tell you to increase the structure by establishing clear rules about when, where, and how he should complete his homework. This would help you create Purposeful Structure. And maybe it would 'work' if indeed there ARE too many other things competing for his time and attention, i.e. the GAF was too high for him.

But, as with most of parenting, it's not that simple. The reason we look for answers about rules and structure as a matter of fact is to lower the Gray Area Factor for ourselves!

Maybe there aren't too many other things competing for your son's time and attention. Maybe he is bored with the homework, i.e. the GAF is too low. Or maybe he doesn't understand the homework which is a different GAF issue that calls for a different response from you.

There are no absolutes about structure and how to make it **Just Right**. It would not be true to say more structure is good and less structure is bad, or visa versa. The Gray Area Factor helps us understand what we're referring to when we say "handling it" and "not handling it". And as a result, we can make better decisions.

As shown in the above example, it's not even a fixed truth that when our kids can't handle something we simply need to increase the structure.

The GAF enables you to "Walk 13 steps in their Nikes"
(Strategy 22)

Knowing what it feels like when the GAF is too high or too low gives us a better understanding of what our kids might be experiencing. We know, for example, what it feels like when we are not given enough choice or when we have too many decisions to make.

Understanding the GAF lowers our frustration and confusion which reduces the possibility that we react to a situation out of anger. The more we understand about a situation, the better able we are to stand in the Reality as we make decisions about structure.

Section 5: Purposeful Structure

> ### FAQ: (cont.)
>
> ### The GAF helps you "Let them have it"
> (Strategy 21)
>
> In the very beginning, there is just us and them. We provide the structure our kids need with no outside interference. Then, before we barely have time to get accustomed to that adventure and responsibility, our kids GROW and their world expands. And with that our jobs get more complicated.
>
> Our kids begin interacting with more people. They are exposed to more messages about right and wrong, good and bad. They receive information from a variety of sources. They begin to see possibilities and opportunities beyond the family. Those adorable little babies start having ideas and opinions of their own.
>
> All this growing up increases the Gray Area Factor, the degree of complexity and uncertainty our kids face. And this expanding GAF occurs alongside the development of our kids' Internal Structure. Our kids get better and better at handling complexity and uncertainty.
>
> Understanding 'growing up' in terms of the GAF helps us make more effective decisions about when and how to give our kids increased responsibility. We use the GAF to assess just how much responsibility our kids can and can't handle.
>
> ### The GAF lets you "Untangle the Feelings" & "Aim Your Control"
> (Strategies 10 and 25)
>
> One of the most frightening things as a parent is that so much of the expanding Gray Area Factor our kids face is beyond our control. And this sends our GAF soaring. And when our GAF is too high we race towards the Illusion and grab for whatever we can to feel in control and in charge.
>
> Understanding the GAF can help us not get blind-sided by our own **Catch 22s**.
>
> ### A Story
>
> > Sarah asked if she could go to Europe for the summer. My fears, based on a high GAF (all the uncertainties involved), had me wanting to tell her no, she could not go.
> >
> > Understanding what my "no" was based upon enabled me to reassess my answer and give more consideration to what would be best for her. I was in a better position to take into account how much uncertainty and complexity she could handle given her Internal Structure.

Aim Your Control, Control Your Aim.

> **FAQ:** (cont.)
>
> **The GAF is a framework (a paradigm) for knowing our kids and making decisions. It gives us an expanded perspective for understanding the decisions we make and those that our kids make.**

In fact, the GAF can help you understand the decisions you make about the strategies in Section 4...

1. As you worked through **Create the Reality,** did any of the strategies strike you as terrible, unthinkable, or completely unusable?

2. For each one that did, consider the Gray Area Factor:

   a. Did the strategy raise the GAF too high for you?

   - If yes, describe how.

   - Identify ways you could modify the strategy to lower its GAF impact on you. Hint: Stop thinking in terms of either-or;
      Either I can use this strategy **or** I can't...

   b. Did you feel the strategy would raise the GAF too high for your kids?

   - If yes, describe how.

   - Identify ways you could modify the strategy to lower its GAF impact on your kids. (Again, bust open your either-or thinking!)

Section 5: Purposeful Structure

> A-ha 5:6

The Primary Adjustment Tools

The Primary Adjustment Tools[7] are Key Elements of the Structure Continuum.

1. **Feedback/Messages**
2. **Rules/Expectations**
3. **Options**
4. **Outcomes**

We use these tools to increase and decrease structure, i.e. to shift along the Structure Continuum.

Example

Increasing the structure with the Rules/Expectations Tool (#2)

The Rule: "I expect you to be home at a reasonable hour."

This rule tells your son that he can't stay out all night. His Internal Structure isn't sufficient to manage the Gray Area Factor created by the situation. You have increased the structure and filled in this gap by eliminating the need for him to make this decision.

And as we practiced in Section 3, **Continuums: Busting Open Either-Or,** each of these Key Elements can be further expanded by thinking of them as sub-continuums with these Key Elements:

a. **Clarity/Explicitness**
b. **Frequency**
c. **Predictability/Preparation**

> **We increase the level of structure by amplifying these Key Elements with respect to the Adjustment Tools.**
>
> **We decrease the level of structure by reducing these Key Elements with respect to the Adjustment Tools.**

---

[7] The Adjustment Tools do overlap but for instructional purposes we'll discuss them as separate and distinct. Irma will help you integrate them to realize their full potential.

Example

Increasing the structure even more with the Key Elements of the Rules/Expectations Tool

The Rule: "I expect you to be home at a reasonable hour."

We can increase the structure (lower the GAF) further to fill in larger gaps by adjusting the Rules/Expectation Tool with its Key Elements:

a. Clarity/Explicitness:

"I expect you to be home by midnight."

Your son does not have to judge what a reasonable hour feels like to him or guess what it means to you.

b. Frequency:

You repeat the expectation each time he goes out rather than just on his 17th birthday when the rule went into effect. He does not have to remember each time he goes out with his friends what the rule is.

c. Predictability/Preparation

You continue defining a reasonable time as midnight. That makes it predictable. Your son does not have to wonder each time he goes out what time he is to be home. It is what he expects. It is easy to remember.

When you modify the structure (to keep it at **Just Right**) by changing the definition of reasonable time, you make sure you tell him ahead of time. If, for example, he has to be up early the next morning, you **prepare** him for the change of what is a reasonable hour. You don't shout out to him as he's walking out the door on Saturday night, "By the way, I want you home at 10:30 tonight."

Prepared for the change, he might still get angry or disagree with it, but he won't be caught off guard and left trying to figure out (high GAF) why it changed or what's wrong with mom. Preparation for change keeps things predictable.

Section 5: Purposeful Structure

Each of the Adjustment Tools can be used as both a Prevention Tool and an Intervention Tool.

As Prevention Tools

We use them to establish a framework within which our kids operate. As part of this framework we determine how much the Tools need to be adjusted by the Key Elements: Clarity/Specificity, Frequency, Predictability/Preparation, in order to keep the environment as close to **Just Right** as possible.

As Intervention Tools

Something happens that calls for a shift in the Purposeful Structure we are providing. We decide which Tools and/or Key Elements will bring the structure back to the hypothetical 100% given the new dynamics.

By keeping the **GAF** and **Just Right** in mind, we are in a better position to avoid overreacting and increasing the structure up to 200%.

(As in grounding our daughter for the rest of her life because she got into trouble at school!)

> Aim Your Control, Control Your Aim.

A-ha 5:7

The Feedback/Message Tool

We modify the structure with The Feedback/Message Tool by sharing our feelings, values, and APES with our kids.

As pointed out at the beginning of this section, everything we say and don't say, do and don't do, impacts our kids' environment. That's because all of it provides feedback and sends messages. We can purposefully adjust the structure, modify the environment, by choosing the feedback we'll give and the messages we'll send.

Examples

Verbal Feedback with implied Messages

- "Thank you for helping fix dinner."
- "You did a great job on your science project."
- "I can't believe you won't go with me to visit your uncle."
- "I love spending time with you."

Non-verbal Messages that give Feedback

- The drawing hanging on the refrigerator
- A hug, a smile
- A dirty look, a frown
- Being too busy to notice the sadness, happiness, pride, frustration…

Feedback/Message Tips

- ✓ When giving feedback, choose your timing based upon your GAF needs and where you are standing on the Control Continuum. (Use Strategy 4 **Stop the action and regroup**.)

- ✓ Pay attention to how and when your kids prefer feedback and use this to improve your delivery and their acceptance.

- ✓ Explore ways to make the 'hard' feedback and tough truths more palatable WITHOUT making them less clear.

- ✓ Remember to give feedback on both process and product as needed, i.e. on what your kids accomplish and on the effort they put into accomplishing it.

- ✓ Watch for clashes between how feedback/messages are intended and how they are received. (Strategy 9 **Check in, check out** can help.)

- ✓ Notice hidden APES that send unintended messages to your kids.

Section 5: Purposeful Structure

Exercise 5:7

1. Identify three ways you could give your daughter feedback or send a message about her choice of friends.

   Describe how you could increase the structure with each of the Key Elements.

   a. Clarity/Explicitness

   b. Frequency

   c. Predictability/Preparation

2. Write down three of the most important messages you want to get across to your kids.

   a. Choose one message and pay attention to all the different ways your feedback either supports or distorts this message.

   b. Notice how you can use the Key Elements to shift the feedback to enhance the message and diminish the distortions.

   c. How do these shifts affect you and your kids?

What helps you accept feedback?

What makes it harder for you to accept feedback?

As parents, we give a lot of unsolicited feedback. It's our job.

The dynamics change when feedback is unsolicited.

What do you want to remember when giving your kids feedback they haven't asked for but need?

Aim Your Control, Control Your Aim.

> A-ha 5:8

The Rules/Expectations Tool

We modify the structure with The Rules/Expectations Tool
by defining the Do's and Don'ts for our kids' behavior.

Rules are declared Expectations. Expectations are implied Rules.

Examples

- On school days, bedtime is 8:00.
- You can only drive with two other kids in the car.
- There will be no piercing or tattoos.
- You may not go to parties if there is no adult in the house.
- You can't have dessert if you haven't eaten your dinner.
- If you use the last ice cube, refill the tray.
- Kids greet adults using the adult's surname.
- As part of this family, everyone does their share.

Rules/Expectations Tips

✓ Limit the number of Rules to those your kids actually need.

✓ Recognize when it's your fear calling the shots and choose whether to act upon it or not.

✓ Be consistent but not rigid. Leave room for mitigating circumstances that call for a change. And when the Rules/Expectations do change, **Put it on the table** (Strategy 3)

✓ Know which Expectations should be stated as Rules. Sometimes kids need things clearly spelled out and sometimes they are successful with a less structured guideline of what you expect.

✓ Help your kids understand the "Why's of Rules and Expectations"

- Why this is a Rule/Expectation here but not here
- Why this a Rule/Expectation now but not before
- Why this is a Rule/Expectation for you but not her

Section 5: Purposeful Structure

> **Teaching our kids how Rules/Expectations work
> increases their Internal Structure,
> helps them be more flexible and adaptable,
> and better prepares them for life's uncertainty and complexity.**

Exercise 5:8

1. List the Rules/Expectations in your home and identify:
   a. The Rules that are clearly stated.
   b. The Expectations that are implied.
   c. The Rules/Expectations that serve as Prevention.
   d. The Rules/Expectations that are in place as Interventions.
2. What would your kids say the Rules/Expectations are?
3. How does this level of structure seem to be working?
   a. Are you confused about any of your Expectations?
   b. Are your kids?
   c. Do any of your Expectations need to be stated as Rules?
   d. Do any of your Rules need to be adjusted using the Key Elements either to increase or decrease structure?

What helps you and your kids remember the Rules/Expectations?

How do your Rules/Expectations take into account your kids' individual personalities and the GAF?

Describe the Feedback that your Rules//Expectations give your kids.
What about the Messages they send?

174

A-ha 5:9

The Options Tool

We modify the structure with The Options Tool by controlling the degree of choice and the number of choices our kids have.

Examples

- "Do you want me to remind you about the test?"
- "How much do you want to be involved in the planning?"
- "Do you want cake or ice cream or cookies for dessert?"
- "What time will you be home?"
- "What should we do about that 'F' on your report card?"

Option Tips

- ✓ Get comfortable with both giving options and declaring the bottom line.

- ✓ Remember that the bottom line can include options and that those options can be stated or implied. Example: The bottom line is you can either go with me or stay in and study. "You may not go to the basketball game" might or might not be said.

- ✓ Identify when your kids are picking up on unintended options, "you didn't say I couldn't", and adjust the structure as needed.

- ✓ Recognize the different level of structure between open-ended options, "What do you want for dinner?", and offering specific choices, "Do you want veggie burgers or steak?"

- ✓ Offer only 'real' choices. Choices you can live with and accept no matter which one your child selects.

- ✓ Increase the structure by allowing your kids fewer options and decrease the structure by allowing them more.

- ✓ Assume your kids hate to be told. Ask instead and build in choice whenever you can.

Section 5: Purposeful Structure

> **Giving kids choices empowers them and helps them develop an effective decision-making process.**

Exercise 5:9

1. Restate each of the following options twice: first in a way that increases the Gray Area Factor and then in a way that decreases it.

    a. Do you want help with your science or your math homework?

    b. Do you want to be a doctor or a lawyer when you grow up?

    How have you used the Key Elements with each one to increase and decrease the structure?

2. Name five ways you currently modify the structure using the Options Tool.

3. Identify a situation in which you either didn't give your kids options they could have handled or gave them choices that were too limiting for them.

    Note: *GAF too low, Too much structure*

4. Identify a situation in which you gave your kids too many or unclear options.

    Note: *GAF too high, Too little structure*

Where would your kids like to have more choice?

Given their GAF needs, where should your kids have more choice?

―――◊―――

Where should they have fewer choices?

―――◊―――

What Messages are you sending with your use of the Options Tool?

―――◊―――

How can you incorporate Options into your Rules/Expectation?

―――◊―――

176

Aim Your Control, Control Your Aim.

A-ha 5:10

The Outcomes Tool

We modify the structure with the Outcomes Tool by determining what occurs as a result of our kids' choices/behaviors.

Examples

- Finish your homework and then you can go outside.
- I'll give you your allowance when you've completed your chores.
- Go to your room.
- If you come home late, your curfew will be reduced by one hour for a month.

Outcome Tips

✓ Recognize those outcomes ("If this, then this...") that are stated and those that are implied.

✓ Be clear about which specific-kid behaviors and kid-APES you want to impact.

✓ Understand that the impact of the Outcome resides "in the eyes of the beholder." Example: If your kid doesn't enjoy reading, taking away that privilege as a consequence for something your child did will not achieve your goals.

✓ Turn off the Automatic Pilot in order to make the most of NATURAL CONSEQUENCES. Examples: A lower grade for not doing homework, missing the school bus because of dawdling, losing a friend as a result of disloyalty.

- Sometimes there are reasons to 'protect' our kids from natural consequences. That's part of Purposeful Structure.
- And sometimes natural consequences present us with our own GAF dilemma.

Natural consequences are not always predictable. The term 'natural' can mean 'come what may'... We don't always know what the natural consequences will be. We don't always know how extensively they will impact.

Examples: How low will the grade go? What will happen if she misses the school bus too many times? How else will losing this friend affect his social life?

So we do all we can to prevent them from occurring even when they are in our children's best interest. Being aware of and facing our fear helps us make the right decisions.
(Use A-ha 3:8 **Those Pesky WhatIfs**, page 67)

Section 5: Purposeful Structure

> **Purposeful Structure includes introducing and allowing for a lack of predictability to prepare our kids for all the curve balls life will throw their way.**
> **This is part of "Room for Growth".**

Exercise 5:10

1. You want your son to stop giving away his lunch at school.

    a. Identify five Outcomes statements, "If this, then this" you could use to address this behavior.

    b. Describe how you would increase the structure for each statement using the Key Elements:

          Clarity/Explicitness

          Frequency

          Predictability/Preparations

2. Identify Outcomes you have in place right now:

    a. Five implied "If this… then this…"

    b. Five stated "If this… then this…"

    c. Is the behavior that is upsetting you most covered by one of these Outcome statements?

    Note: If a behavior is upsetting you, it is not meeting your Expectations. How clear are you on what that Expectation is? How clearly have you shared that with your child?

    d. How could you increase the structure to further impact that behavior?

What Outcomes do you tend to rely on most?

Identify 10 more Outcomes you could use.

Describe how Outcomes are a form of Feedback and how they send Messages.

Describe how Outcomes can be incorporated into Rules and Expectations.

Describe how you could use the Options Tool to define Outcomes.

Aim Your Control, Control Your Aim.

A-ha 5:11

What to Look For

Here are some indicators that you might need to provide more Purposeful Structure. These are signs that the gap between what our kids can handle and the Gray Area Factor our kids are facing isn't effectively being filled:

- Our kids are having difficulty delaying gratification. They keep going for the immediate "feel good" and end up in hot water.
- Our kids are having difficulty 'reading' what's going on, choosing what to attend to, or prioritizing effectively.
- Our kids are having trouble controlling their impulses.
- Our kids are 'acting out' as their primary, or only, way to deal with overwhelming emotions such as anger, frustration, or sadness.
- Our kids are not successfully learning the intended lesson.

Our own APES and actions also help us know when we need to provide more structure:

- We have a strong belief that our kids' needs are not being met but can't put our finger on why or how.
- We have the overwhelming feeling that we don't know what our kids need.
- We keep reacting from anger, fear, and frustration.

All of the above are great indicators that there is not enough structure. To complicate matters even further however, they could also be signs that we are providing too much Purposeful Structure.

Exercise 5:11

1. Describe how each indicator could demonstrate that there is too much structure and the Gray Area Factor is too low for our kids.
2. For each indicator that rings true in your home right now:
   - What specific **behaviors** lead you to this assumption, feeling, or conclusion?
   - How are you already addressing these behaviors?
   - What has been effective so far and what hasn't?
   - Do these indicators reflect there is too much or too little structure?
   - Identify three other ways you could address each behavior using the Primary Adjustment Tools.

179

Section 5: Purposeful Structure

A-ha 5:12

Questions to Ask Yourself

Some questions you can ask yourself to determine if you are providing **too little structure** for your kids (if the Gray Area Factor they face is too high).

1. Is there too much uncertainty?
2. Are there too many choices?
3. Are my expectations unclear?
4. Am I sending mixed-messages?
5. Is she/he having a tough time making decisions?
6. Are there too many distractions?
7. ?
8. ?

Exercise 5:12

1. Add more questions to the above list.
2. List some questions that would help determine if you are providing **too much structure**.
3. As demonstrated in "What to Look For", too much structure and too little structure might look the same in terms of how our kids respond.
   - Identify five ways you could use the **Create the Reality Strategies** to help you decide if there is too much or too little structure.

We maximize our sense of control and our kids' sense of control by having the structure at *Just Right*.

> Aim Your Control, Control Your Aim.

A-ha 5:13

Tying It All Together

The **Create the Reality Strategies** are part of **Purposeful Structure**. The more we understand how, the better able we are to integrate the Strategies into our parenting.

These Strategies:

- Give **Feedback** and send **Messages** to our kids
- Can be used to establish **Rules**, express **Expectations**, determine **Outcomes**, and define **Options**
- Facilitate our understanding of what our kids need with respect to the **Gray Area Factor** and help us meet those needs

Here are some examples of ways in which the Strategies, the GAF, and Purposeful Structure are interwoven:

Strategy 1
Shift to a Learning Stance

- We can use Expansion Questions to help us decide when to modify the structure and whether it needs increasing or decreasing.
- When we accept that we don't have all the answers, it is easier for our kids to teach us what is **Just Right** for them.

Strategy 2
Let them have it

- We use **Internal Structure** and the **Gray Area Factor** to determine what responsibilities our kids are ready for.
- We shift the structure towards **Just Right** by giving our kids the appropriate responsibilities.

Strategy 3
Put it on the table

- When there is an exception to the **Rule** and we put it on the table, we provide **Clarity** and **Predictability**.
- When we share our feelings and APES with our kids (give them this **Feedback**) they don't have to guess. They are faced with less uncertainty.

Section 5: Purposeful Structure

- Telling our kids how the **Gray Area Factor** affects us (sharing our fear of the unknown, of being confused by too many factors or too much going on) helps them learn about their own **GAF** needs.
- What we choose to put on the table affects the **GAF** for our kids. Some of our **Feedback** might raise the level of uncertainty and complexity too high for them. When we understand this, we are better able to choose what we will and won't put on the table.

Strategy 4

Stop the action and regroup

- We can stop the action and regroup when the **Gray Area Factor** is too much for us or our kids.
- Regrouping can include assessing our own and our kids' **GAF** needs.

Strategy 5

Lighten up

- When the **Gray Area Factor** is too high or too low, either for us or our kids, it can be really tough to Lighten up. Understanding this can help us come up with a plan to regain balance and perspective.
- Our fear of the unknown, the **Gray Area Factor**, impacts how tightly we hold on to our agendas and how much slack we can cut ourselves and our kids.

Strategy 6

Let it go

- We sometimes have a hard time Letting it go as we try to lower the GAF for our kids. We want them to 'get it'. Letting it go can be hard for us to do as it raises the GAF for us. We are less certain about what our kids understand.

Strategy 7

Pull the plug on non-productive patterns

- Non-productive patterns are often a **GAF** issue. The **GAF** is too high or too low for our kids but we don't understand which it is so we keep saying and doing the same things that don't work.
- Looking for non-productive patterns as a product of **GAF** issues can help us recognize and pull the plug on them.

Strategy 8

Assess the nag level

- Instead of nagging, we can explore ways to adjust the structure to get what we want. "How can I use **Rules**, **Options**, or **Outcomes** to change this?"

Strategy 9
Check in, check out

- When we check out what we are observing or assuming about our kids, we don't have to guess what's going on with them. This lowers our **GAF**.
- When we check in with our own APES and feelings, we don't have to guess why we respond the way we do. This lowers our **GAF** and allows us to Pull the plug on non-productive patterns.

Strategy 10
Untangle the feelings

- We can determine if our own **GAF** needs are compelling us to protect our kids from Natural Consequences.
- We can determine if our own **GAF** needs are interfering with making effective decisions about what our kids need in terms of **Rules, Options**, and **Outcomes**.

Strategy 11
Word problems, go figure!

- Identifying a dilemma as a word problem takes the uncertainty out of other things that might be going on and what we need to do about them. It lowers our **GAF**.

Strategy 12
Explain the bottom line

- Explaining the bottom line clarifies our reasons so our kids don't have to guess. It lowers their **GAF**.
- We can Explain the bottom line with respect to **Rules, Options**, and **Outcomes**.

Strategy 13
Stop trying to fix & solve, just listen

- Listening, without the agenda to fix and solve, can help us determine if there is a **GAF** issue that needs addressing.

Strategy 14
Just love 'em

- Just love 'em is a great way to really be there for our kids when things get scary, when the **GAF** gets too high for them.
- Just being reminded that we are there for our kids can lower their **GAF**.

Section 5: Purposeful Structure

Strategy 15
The butterfly and the bull

- Our **GAF** impacts our responses. Going for over-kill with **Outcomes**, i.e. stopping all extra-curricular activities for a year because your child broke a **Rule**, is the Bull.
- Adjusting the structure in appropriate increments is the Butterfly.

Strategy 16
Co-design

- We can co-design **Rules/Expectations**, **Options**, **Outcomes**, and a system for **Feedback**.
- It's harder for kids to complain about the structure when they are part of planning it.
- **Internal Structure** is full of wisdom, regardless of the age of the kid.
  Co-designing allows us to tap into all that marvelous wisdom.
- Sometimes our kids struggle for input, for more control, and Co-designing shifts the structure to **Just Right** by allowing our kids more input.
- We can use Co-designing as a way to teach our kids how to effectively deal with more **Options** and less **Predictability**.
- Co-designing sends our kids great **Messages**.

Strategy 17
Reframe it

- Our understanding of the **Gray Area Factor** enables us to reframe our interpretation of our kids' behaviors and choices.
- We can intentionally reframe the **Outcomes** to build in success.

Strategy 18
Use the Back Door

- Giving our kids **Options** is one way to go in the Back Door. This decrease in structure can break an impasse.

Strategy 19
You're right, I can't make you

- Admitting this can raise the **Gray Area Factor** higher than our kids know they are ready for. As much as they might want to prove it, hearing us say it could introduce enough of the unknown to be scary. At times this might not be a bad thing…
- Putting this on the table can raise our **GAF** since we don't know how far our kids will take this admission and exactly what they will do with it.

Strategy 20
Turn off that automatic no

- When we turn off our automatic no we can make better decisions based on the development of our kids' **Internal Structures** and the level of **uncertainty** and **complexity** involved.

Strategy 21
Unscramble the issues

- This strategy lowers the **GAF** for everyone as it adds certainty and clarity.

Strategy 22
Walk 13 steps in their Nikes

- We might not have done 'that' ourselves, but understanding 'that' helps us stand in the Reality and make more effective decisions about **Options**, **Rules**, and **Outcomes**. We know what it's like when the **Gray Area Factor** is too high or too low and when there is not enough or too much structure.

Strategy 23
Think smaller

- Related to the Butterfly and the Bull, the **GAF** keeps us from overreacting when the structure needs modifying.
- With respect to **Feedback**, **Rules**, and **Outcomes**, we should think in terms of the smallest steps and the shortest terms that will have the impact we want.

Strategy 24
Hang in there

- We can use our understanding of the **GAF** and knowledge of what our kids are able to independently handle to determine if we are meeting our kids' need. This helps us decide if we should hang in there and wait for them to come on board or if we should modify what we are doing.

Strategy 25
Aim your control... Control your aim

- This strategy is all about lowering the **Gray Area Factor** for ourselves in effective ways so we don't race towards the Illusion.

Section 5: Purposeful Structure

| A-ha 5:14 |

Four More Purposeful Structure Tips

Tip #1
Some inappropriate kid behaviors indicate an inability to organize time, 'stuff', thoughts, or physical space.

The Primary Adjustment Tools can be used to impact behaviors that result from disorganization. Using them with high levels of Clarity/Specificity, Frequency, and Predictability/Preparation, helps compensate for a lack of organization.

But sometimes they aren't enough...

Example

> Dave comes home late from basketball practice nearly every day. His family waits for him and dinner gets cold. Mom has tried giving him additional privileges when he makes it on time (The **Outcomes** Tool); reminding him each morning what time he needs to be home (The **Rules/Expectations** Tool); giving him the choice of having dinner be served at 5:30 or 6:00 (The **Options** Tool).
>
> Dave is still late most evenings. After practice, he can't find his street shoes in his gym locker, he gets side-tracked in conversations, and he forgets to check the clock.

We can also modify the structure with **Organization Tools**: Check lists, monitoring systems, written schedules, calendars, timers, written reminders, verbal prompts...

Recognizing which behaviors result from disorganization helps us make better decisions about which Tools to use.

- Which of your kids' behaviors may be a result of disorganization rather than deliberate non-compliance?
- How could you use **Shift to a Learning Stance** (Strategy 1) and **Check in, Check out** (Strategy 9) to find out?
- If they are a result of disorganization, how could you modify the existing structure?
- Which **Create the Reality Strategies** could you use to help your child understand what's going on?

Tip #2

Not every behavior we perceive as difficult needs to be changed or calls for a structure modification.

A Story

I picked up Katie for a morning meeting. I knew she was nervous. I knew she needed me to be there for her... available but QUIET. She is not a Morning Person.

I wanted to hold her hand as reassurance. As it was, I put my hand on her leg and she very subtly moved it away. Sometimes when Katie is tense, she doesn't want to be touched.

With Sarah, this scenario would have been different. She would have gotten into the car talking and would have held my hand the whole way.

What I've noticed is that as long as my own fears and comfort level don't muddy the water, neither response is easier or harder, more or less acceptable...

When we recognize our kids as individuals, separate from us and each other, we are far more effective at determining what is a problem and what is just different.

Sometimes it's our Perspective that needs shifting.

- Identify which kid behaviors are hard for you to deal with.
- For each one decide:
    Do I need to modify the structure to address this behavior?
    Do I need to **Lighten up** and accept this as part of my child's uniqueness?
- How could these **Create the Reality Strategies** help?
    - **Untangle the feelings** (Strategy 10)
    - **Stop trying to fix & solve, just listen** (Strategy 13)
    - **Walk 13 steps in their Nikes** (Strategy 22)
    - **Aim your control... Control your Aim** (Strategy 25)

Section 5: Purposeful Structure

Tip #3

Value and cherish your kids' uniqueness even as you provide structure and set limits to help them 'fit in' with the rest of the world.

Example

The 6-year-old who insists that you knock before entering her room, that she be called by her full name, allowed to pour the juice, and choose her own cereal. The little girl who will only wear dresses in varying shades of blue.

We call her stubborn. We call her uncompromising. We call her strong-willed. We can also call her confident, self-aware, and independent.

How do we cherish and value this little girl's strengths while we're worrying about giving in to her every whim and spoiling her? How do we acknowledge her preferences without raising an inflexible child?

She most likely will hit the phase 'I'm too (fat, thin, smart, dumb, ugly, different)' in the not-so-distant future. It's our job to help her get there with her strong sense of self still intact.

- Which kid trait or tendency do you worry about?
- How will this trait or tendency help them navigate their world? (**Reframe it**, Strategy 17)
- How do you want to modify the structure given Tip #3?

Tip #4

Don't Lose the Forest through the Trees

A-ha Parenting is not losing sight of the Forest, the Big Picture, as we create Purposeful Structure.

To see the Big Picture we need to

1. Slow down enough to grasp what's really going on.
2. Disengage from the details and the muck long enough to ask Big Picture Expansion Questions such as:

   ➢ What do I want to accomplish with this feedback, this rule, this consequence, or this strategy?

   ➢ How does addressing this behavior fit in with what I really want for my child?

   ➢ Are the ripped jeans worth arguing about or is getting to the doctor's appointment on time more important?

A Tip about this Tip

**The details and the Big Picture tend to shift and change places.
Coming from Intentional Self is crucial for
choosing our focus and prioritizing at any given moment.**

- Choose three Rules you have for your kids.
- State the Big Picture each Rule serves.
- Consider how these **Create the Reality Strategies** can help you focus and prioritize.

  - **Lighten up** (Strategy 5)
  - **Let it go** (Strategy 6)
  - **Just love 'em** (Strategy 14)
  - **The butterfly and the bull** (Strategy 15)

Section 5: Purposeful Structure

Purposeful Structure Check In

Describe how each of the following provides an answer for those questions you identified on page 154:

The Gray Area Factor

Internal Structure

The Hypothetical 100% Principle

The Primary Adjustment Tools

Put it all Together

Describe how **Purposeful Structure** relies on **Intentional Self** and visa versa.

Describe how **Purposeful Structure** helps you stand in the **Reality** and how standing in the **Reality** helps you create **Purposeful Structure**.

Describe how the A-ha's in Section 3, **In Charge of Me**, will help you implement what you've learned about the **Gray Area Factor** and **Purposeful Structure**.

Example:
I need to **Pay Attention** to find out if I am providing the right amount of structure. What I **Pay Attention** to sends messages and provides feedback to my kids.

Notes

We can't make a sunflower seed grow into a snapdragon
but we sure can do everything within our power to give it
the soil, water, and nutrients it needs to grow
into the best darn sunflower it can be.

Same thing with providing the love and the structure our kids need…

Section 6

Power Struggles

Power Struggles can only occur with two participants...

If we refuse to play, our kids have nothing to push against.

Section 6: Power Struggles

Last but certainly not least

Your body tenses. Your heart races. Your face reddens. It's getting harder and harder to breathe. **YOU WANT TO BE HEARD.**

So your voice gets louder and louder, the pitch goes up, and the words rush out seemingly with a life of their own.

You find yourself in a shouting match where the spoils go to the one who gets the last word in… edgewise or otherwise… at any cost. And all of this is happening to your child too.

OR… It's very quiet. The silence weighed down by recrimination, resistance and anger. The heels dug in. No room to move. No room for understanding. No budging from this point of view, opinion, or position.

You find yourself in a Battle of the Wills where you and your child hold on tighter and tighter until one of you bursts.

Ah, Power Struggles…

> **What fuels 'em?**

Fear, anger, Catch 22s, Automatic Pilot…. Getting so caught up in our agendas that the forest is obliterated by the trees.

> **Who needs 'em?**

No one because, if played out all the way, the outcome is always the same. Everyone loses. Whether it's losing face, dignity, trust, or confidence, your sense of well-being and balance, everyone always loses something, even the 'winner'.

> **Who can avoid 'em?**

We all can when we stand in the Reality with our Automatic Pilots turned off.

Aim Your Control, Control Your Aim.

P.S. 6:1

Avoiding Power Struggles

> Step 1: Recognize the Wall
> Step 2: Stop the Action
> Step 3: See the Kid
> Step 4: Change Direction

Step 1: Recognize the Wall.

- "Yes, but… Yes, but… Yes, but…"
- "That won't work."
- "I've already tried that."
- "You don't understand."
- "I can't… No, I can't…"
- "You never…"
- "You always…"
- Eyes rolling around in their sockets
- Interruptions
- Refusal to speak
- Going off on tangents

We need to notice the signs, phrases, word patterns, and other cues that indicate our child is not hearing us at the moment, that we are simply not getting through.

195

Section 6: Power Struggles

Examples

A
Dad: She has to be given a chance. Why don't you just go in and talk to her.

Steve: It won't make a difference.

Dad: Have you tried?

Steve: No, but it won't work.

Dad: Tell her what really happened.

Steve: Dad, she's not going to listen.

> **Steve is not open to what dad is suggesting, what dad is advising.**

B
Mom: Go apologize to your sister.

Greg: She started it.

Mom: I don't care. You're older and you know better.

Greg: She can't come in my room.

Mom: Okay, but she needed the phone and you weren't around.

Greg: She just walks in and starts going through my stuff.

Mom: I know but…

Greg: You always give in to her.

> **Greg is interrupting and moving into a bigger, tangential issue.**

C
Dad: You're late for school. Let's get moving.

Lorrie: I'm not going.

Dad: Yes you are.

Lorrie: No I'm not.

Dad: You don't have a choice in the matter.

Lorrie: I don't care. You can't make me.

> **Lorrie has dug her heels in and played the trump card…**

Step 2: Stop the Action

Stop trying to teach or advise. Stop trying to make your point. Check in with YOU. Ask yourself some Expansion Questions:

- *What am I trying to accomplish?*
- *How frustrated do I feel?*
- *What attitude am I conveying with my body language and words?*
- *What am I reacting to?*
- *Is this conversation moving forward?*
- *Is either of us saying anything new?*
- *What am I afraid of?*
- *How rigid am I being?*
- *What am I missing or not understanding?*

Step 3: See the Kid

Open up to and understand what might be going on from your child's perspective. To do this you need to:

- Let go of your agenda
- Stop assuming that you know what's going on with them
- Stop deciding whether they are right or wrong or if what they feel is good or bad
- Get truly curious about what your child needs
- Listen to what they are saying and notice what they are not saying

Step 4: Change Direction

Examples

- **Shift to a Learning Stance:**

    "What makes this so important to you?"

    "What is making you so angry or frustrated with me?"

    "What aren't I getting?"

    "Is there a different way you can explain this to me?"

Section 6: Power Struggles

- **Let Them Have Responsibility for What's Next:**

    "What do you think would help get us back in sync?"

    "This is a mess. How do we get out of here?"

- **Put it on the Table:**

    "It feels like I'm not understanding what you're trying to tell me."

    "This feels silly. There has to be a different way for us to talk about this."

    "I agree with you here… This is the part I don't get and where I need your help."

- **Stop the Action to Regroup but Leave the Door Open:**

    "This doesn't seem to be working. I'm going back in the kitchen. Let me know when you want to try this conversation again."

    "My answer is no and I'm not sure how to help you accept that. I'll be in the living room if you need further clarification, as long as the questions are new ones!"

- **Lighten up, Inside and Out:**

    "Whew, I don't know about you but this is hard work. I could really use a lemonade break right about now. I love you and don't have a clue where to go with this."

FAQ: But how do I know when to change directions?

How long do we try to get our kids to listen? How far should we go to demonstrate that we want to hear what they have to say? How do we know when we have stepped over the line and into a power struggle?

Inevitably, this is another on-the-spot judgment.

The more you shift towards Intentional Self and understand your Catch 22s, the better you will get at recognizing the "Brick Wall Here" signs. And the more you practice noticing the signs, the easier it will get to change directions before you're engaged in a full blown power struggle.

Exercise 6:1

1. Describe the last Brick Wall you encountered.

    a. How did you know it was a Brick Wall?

    b. What were the signs?

    c. If you changed direction, what did you do?

    d. If you didn't, what kept you moving straight ahead?

2. Go on a Brick Wall Hunt

    a. Pay Attention each time you are simply not getting through.

    b. For each scenario, describe what the signs were.

    c. Jot down any patterns that you notice with respect to specific issues or kids.

    d. Record which strategies you tried and how they worked.

    e. If they didn't work, what else could you have tried?

Section 6: Power Struggles

P.S. 6:2

Disengaging from Power Struggles

> Step 1: Read the Indicators
> Step 2: Choose Not to Participate
> Step 3: Focus on Right Now
> Step 4: Step off the Ladder

Okay, so you missed the initial signs, you came to the Brick Wall and instead of changing direction, **YOU TRIED TO CRASH RIGHT THROUGH IT!**

Power Struggles are about escalation and escalation feeds on itself. It's like climbing a ladder. You start on one rung… your child moves to the rung above you… you move to the one above that… she/he moves to the one above that…

Example

Mom: No. You can't go.

Sue: Why not?

Mom: Because you're too young.

Sue: Yeah, but Sally's mom is letting her go

Mom: I don't care what Sally's mom is doing. I can't let you go.

Sue: You can't or won't?

Mom: We've been through this before. Fourteen is too young to go out on dates.

Sue: But I've already gone to parties where I'm alone with boys.

Mom: When? What do you mean?

Sue: Last weekend.

Mom: What did you do? What happened? What are you talking about?

Sue: We were playing this game…

Mom: I knew I couldn't trust you.

Sue: Everyone is going. You are so stupid.

Mom: Don't you dare talk to me that way.

Sue: Why? It's how you talk to me.

Mom: Don't get fresh with me young lady. You do this every time I tell you no and I'm tired of it. I won't put up with it anymore.

Sue: I hate you.

Mom: Well guess what…

> **To end a power struggle, someone has to step off the ladder…**

Step 1: Read the Indicators

- Neither of you are hearing a word the other is saying
- You're both frustrated and perhaps angry
- Nothing new is being said
- You keep talking over each other
- It's no longer about being understood
- Now it's about not backing down, not giving in
- There is no effort on either side to listen or learn
- Both of you are determined to have the 'last word', to 'win'
- Your body shows signs of anger and frustration
- Or… the silence weighs a ton!

Step 2: Choose Not to Participate

- Decide this power struggle is going to end right now
- Let go of the need to 'win'

Step 3: Focus on Right Now

- Stop trying to make your original point
- You can create the time and opportunity to get back to it later
- Remember, nothing can be taught or learned until the power struggle is ended

Section 6: Power Struggles

Step 4: Step off the Ladder

Examples

Each of the 25 Create the Reality Strategies used as an Intervention to Step off the Ladder

- **Strategy 1: Shift to a Learning Stance**

    "What do you suppose will happen if we keep going?"

- **Strategy 2: Let them have it (the responsibility that is)**

    "How do you want to handle this?"

- **Strategy 3: Put it on the table**

    "This sure feels like one of those power struggles that neither of us ever wins."

- **Strategy 4: Stop the action and regroup**

    "I'm walking away right now."

- **Strategy 5: Lighten up**

    "This is one of our better ones, don't you think?"

- **Strategy 6: Let it go**

    This just really isn't worth it. I've lost sight of what really matters.

- **Strategy 7: Pull the plug on non-productive patterns**

    "Every time I try to answer your question, you interrupt me."

- **Strategy 8: Assess the nag level**

    "Which part of what I'm saying feels unreasonable to you?"

- **Strategy 9: Check in, check out**

    Why am I getting pulled into this? My anger doesn't usually get the better of me. I wonder if I'm actually afraid of something. I am. But what?

- **Strategy 10: Untangle the feelings**

    She's upsetting me because she's acting just like Sonny. But she's not Sonny, she's my daughter and I cherish her more than anything else in the world. What does she need from me right now?

Aim Your Control, Control Your Aim.

- **Strategy 11: Word problems, go figure!**

   What's pushing her buttons? What did I say? What's pushing my buttons?

- **Strategy 12: Explain the bottom line**

   "I want you to go to your room. We aren't getting anywhere and I think we'll have a better shot at this if we take a short break."

- **Strategy 13: Stop trying to fix & solve, just listen**

   Action: Close your mouth.

- **Strategy 14: Just love 'em**

   Action: Smile, go for the hug, remind them how much they mean to you.

- **Strategy 15: The butterfly and the bull**

   "I'm wondering if you would consider…"

- **Strategy 16: Reframe it**

   Boy, this is really a hot topic for both of us. I admire her strong sense of fairness. Now how can I acknowledge that and break this impasse?

- **Strategy 17: Co-design**

   "I really want you to hear me. And I understand that you want me to hear you. Do you think it would work if we agreed to take turns, each talking uninterrupted for five minutes?"

- **Strategy 18: Use the backdoor**

   Action: Pretend that the power struggle is over and make your next statement from there.

- **Strategy 19: You're right, I can't make you**

   "You're right. I can't make you."

- **Strategy 20: Turn off that automatic no**

   Yes I CAN *get out of this power struggle right now.*

- **Strategy 21: Unscramble the issues**

   "What is it we're really disagreeing about?"

Section 6: Power Struggles

- **Strategy 22: Walk 13 steps in their Nikes**

    I wonder how frustrated she is that she never gets to...

- **Strategy 23: Think smaller**

    What's one thing I can say right now to diffuse her anger and mine?

- **Strategy 24: Hang in there**

    I hate this. I don't want to do this anymore. I'm tired of fighting with her. I've given it my best shot. Okay, Enough of that... I'll try this and see how it works...

- **Strategy 25: Aim your control... Control your aim**

    I can't change her mind for her. I can't make her get this. I can, however, end this power struggle by...

Identify which examples overlap.

**For each ones that overlap,
identify the other strategies they demonstrate.**

**Over time, as you work with the Create the Reality Strategies,
as they become a fundamental part of your parenting,
they become less separate and distinct.**

Aim Your Control, Control Your Aim.

Exercise 6:2

1. Think of a power struggle you have recently engaged in.

    a. Write out as much of the conversation as you can remember.

    b. Identify the initial Brick Wall.

    c. Identify two ways you could have Changed Direction at that point.

    d. Identify other places where you could have stepped off the ladder and what strategies you could have used.

2. Create a Power Struggle Notebook. Title each page "Hey, that was a Power Struggle". For each entry, describe:

    a. What you were thinking.

    b. What you were feeling.

    c. The Catch 22 involved.

    d. How you could have stepped off the ladder earlier.

    e. What signs you missed.

    f. What compelled you to keep climbing.

    g. What point you absolutely had to make.

    h. What you forgot to remember.

    i. All the things you did well!

Section 6: Power Struggles

P.S. 6:3

A Power Struggle Check List

When faced with a brick wall or engaged in a power struggle, **Stop the action and regroup** by asking yourself these Expansion Questions:

1. What am I trying to control here?
2. What do I want to achieve?
3. What attitude am I expressing?
4. Am I listening to and reading my child?
5. What impact am I having?
6. Whose needs am I responding to?
7. Do I feel calm and centered or out-of-control?
8. What am I afraid of?
9. What am I learning about myself or my child?

The Illusion of Control ←——————————→ The Reality of Control

Our feet are firmly planted in the Reality...

...when we are open to and curious about our kids' APES, feelings, actions, and choices

...when their APES, feelings, actions, and choices help shift us more towards Intentional Self

...when, considering our kids' APES, feelings, actions, and choices, we make a conscious choice about what our next step will be

Aim Your Control, Control Your Aim.
A Final Check In

On a scale of 1 – 10: How much have you gotten out of this workbook?

―――◆―――

On a scale of 1 – 10: How much responsibility have you taken to get what you want?

―――◆―――

What do you now know that you didn't know when you started?

―――◆―――

What did you realize you already knew but are now more aware of?
How will this increased awareness help you be the parent you want to be?

―――◆―――

Which A-ha's and Strategies have become a part of your parenting?

―――◆―――

What's next for you and your kids?

―――◆―――

P.S. Thanks for allowing me to be your partner on this Journey.
- Irma

Aim Your Control, Control Your Aim.
Part of the *A-ha Living* Series

A-ha's are the Insights we get when we Pay Attention.

This workbook provides the foundation for:

- Guided Independent Discovery -

- Individual Coaching –

- Family Coaching -

- Guided Group Discovery Workshops –

I of the Storm Coaching Partnerships,

provides Coaching, Training, and Consultation Services

for individuals, school districts, businesses and social service organizations.

For more information and to purchase additional copies of this book:

andy@mycoachandy.com
www.mycoachandy.com